# SILENT SENTINELS

# SILENT SENTINELS

**The story of Norfolk's fixed defences during the twentieth century**

CHRISTOPHER BIRD

**The Larks Press**

*Published by the Larks Press*
*Ordnance Farmhouse, Guist Bottom, Dereham,*
*Norfolk NR20 5PF*
*01328 829207*
Larks.Press@btinternet.com
Website: www.booksatlarkspress.co.uk

*Printed by the Lanceni Press,*
*Garrood Drive, Fakenham, Norfolk*

*First published November 1999*
*Reprinted 2001, 2008*

*British Library Cataloguing-in-Publication Data*
*A catalogue record for this book is available from the British Library*



Front cover: An Alan Williams turret at Cley-next-the-Sea



*ISBN 978 0 948400 81 1*

---

# *ACKNOWLEDGEMENTS*

---

I should like to thank Mr D.Bailey, Derek Bales, Hubert Dawson, Kim Dowe, Mr R.N.Evans, Alan Lockwood, Derek Manning, Roly Millar, Gwillum Morley, Alan Shaw, Mike Sparkes, Don and Jean Spinks, Martin Stiles (custodian of the Walpole family archives), Mr R.S.Symonds and the late William Stibbons for their help with this project.

The survey which I began in 1990 soon grew into a task of huge proportions as I realised the extent of my undertaking. It soon became clear that to record all of the defences would not be a one-man job, and the survey at the end of this book is a joint effort, combining the work of Peter Kent (who co-ordinated the project), Simon Purcell, Mike Osborne, Philippa Miller and myself. We are greatly indebted to John Wright, who gave us access to archive Norfolk County Council records, thus adding many long-vanished sites to our survey. I should also like to thank the dozens of people who have helped me track down individual sites.

I am extremely grateful to the late Henry Wills, whose pioneering work first prompted me to record the defences, for his help and advice; to Mary Manning, who published the articles I wrote as my work progressed; to my family for their co-operation with the project, even though it ate into their holidays; and in particular to my mother, who drove me to many of the sites and who gave me so much encouragement with what turned out to be a nine-year task.

I am grateful to the Public Record Office, the Trustees of the Imperial War Museum, London, and the Norfolk Archaeological Unit for permission to use illustrations in this book.

All photographs are by the author or Margaret Bird unless otherwise stated.

Christopher Bird

*CONTENTS*

# *FOREWORD*

The danger of an invading force landing in Norfolk is not a new one. The county's proximity to Scandinavia as well as to the Low Countries makes it vulnerable to attack from several possible enemies. It is famous for its flat landscape, and much of its lonely coast is suited to an invading force. Jack Higgins chose to set *The Eagle has Landed* near Blakeney, half-way along the North Norfolk coast.

Professor Ewald Banse wrote a book about the invasion of England, published in English in 1934 as *Germany, Prepare for War!* After listing Holland, Belgium and the north-east coast of France, he stated that a second and even more important region to be occupied was East Anglia, for 'the Great Ouse which flows into the Wash, and a number of streams flowing into the Blackwater Estuary which are separated from the sources of the Ouse by a few miles only, make the peninsula into a regular island which provides an invading army with safe and roomy quarters, from which it can threaten London (which is quite close, and without natural defences on that side), and also the industrial Midlands not far away'.

*Part of Norfolk's coastline, stretching from Weybourne to Sheringham, which was heavily defended in the Second World War (1998)*

Fixed defences against invasion were constructed in Norfolk as long ago as Roman times. Fearing invasion by the Saxons, the Romans built a chain of ten forts from Portsmouth to Brancaster in the fourth century AD. In later years, Norfolk was frequently raided by the Vikings, who then settled there.

In the spring of 1588, the places considered vulnerable to landings by the Spanish were Cley Haven, Weybourne Hope, Waxham, Winterton and Great Yarmouth, where the sea was deep and provided good anchorages.[1]

King's Lynn was, if attacked, to have the causeway at the East Gate cut, the postern gates blocked up, and the banks breached to let the sea surround the town. Other defensive measures included the enlargement of a fort at Weybourne, the building of another at Blakeney, thus protecting Cley Haven, and the cutting of the causeway to the beach at Salthouse.

In addition, inland defences were planned at the key crossings of the rivers: the Little Ouse at Brandon and Thetford; the Bure at Wroxham and Acle; the Ant at the Way Bridge; and the Thurne at Potter Heigham. The thinking of the military planners in 1940 relied on the same principle as that of 1588 - to use the rivers as natural 'stop' lines; Second World War defences were built at all these sites.

Weybourne Hope has long been considered a particularly vulnerable point. The Danes are believed to have landed there on their invasions. By 1781 it was suggested that a new fortification be constructed in view of the risk of attack from France, the *History of Norfolk* noting the strategic importance of the area:

> This Weybourne Hope...is the most dangerous place, and most open to the enemy, of any on the Norfolk coast: the shore is the boldest of any, and transport ships may approach it so very near as almost to land an army without the assistance of flat-bottomed boats.[2]

Fear of a French invasion became more acute with Napoleon in power. In 1803 Major Alexander Bryce, the Commanding Engineer of the Eastern District, carried out a survey of the North Norfolk coast, to assess at which areas troops might be disembarked. Cromer was considered vulnerable, as its battery of 24-pounders could not sweep along the beach, and there were many passages up the cliff by which attacking infantry could ascend. Weybourne, Blakeney, Wells, Holkham, Brancaster and Titchwell Marshes, and King's Lynn were also considered to be good landing places for the enemy.[3]

*Greater importance was given to the defence of Mundesley in the Second World War than in the Napoleonic Wars, as the anti-tank obstacles now piled up at the foot of the cliffs show*[4] *(1998)*

What is surprising about this report is the number of places *not* thought to be worth defending. Happisburgh, Keswick, the area between Cromer and Weybourne, Salthouse, the area between

Blakeney and Wells, Burnham Overy Staithe and Brancaster Staithe were all considered to be free from risk. Almost all these places were defended in the Second World War. In some places the geographical situation had changed, making them more vulnerable. Salthouse Marsh, for example, was entirely under water at the time of the 1803 report, and was described as impassable; by the Second World War it was considered to be worthy of defence and was protected with a 6-inch gun battery, anti-tank blocks and pillboxes. Bryce recommended that at spring tides the neighbouring Cley Marsh, which was drained, might be flooded by raising a sluice in the sea wall at Cley. He visited Mundesley, and one can imagine the residents enthusiastically trying to persuade him that their village required the very heaviest defences, for he concluded that 'Although the inhabitants of this part seem to attach considerable importance to Mundesley, I can hardly bring myself to be of their opinion'!

The pillbox seems to have had its genesis in this period of fortification. In 1798 a captain advising the general commanding the Eastern District about the best means of protecting the coast said, 'Now there are no works that appear to me so likely to effect this general object as a simple tower of brickwork defended by a handful of resolute men'.[5] The captain was in fact talking about the Martello tower, but he might well have been describing its twentieth-century descendants.

**Notes to the Foreword**

[1] Basil Cozens-Hardy, 'Norfolk Coastal Defences in 1588', p 311.

[2] M.J.Armstrong, *History and Antiquities of the County of Norfolk,* p 117.

[3] PRO: WO 30/100, pp 147-163.

[4] TG 3130 3690.

[5] PRO: WO 30/100, p 53. The captain was Thomas Vincent Reynolds.

# THE GREAT WAR

When war was declared in 1914 there was widespread public fear of invasion, fuelled by the huge proliferation of sensational literature on the subject which had been published over the preceding few years. Like Suffolk and Essex, Norfolk received some troops for protection. The troops were stationed at the same places that had been defended in the past, in particular the area from Cley to Sheringham, though much of the coast was considered impenetrable, such as the area around the Wash.

Public alarm increased after the hurried bombardment of Great Yarmouth and Lowestoft on 3rd November 1914. As a result, trenches were dug between Salthouse and Sheringham, and between Hunworth and Briston. The area between Salthouse and Weybourne was heavily protected. In addition to eleven defence positions overlooking the beach, manned by four companies, there were thirty trenches, most of them in a line running from Gallow Hill to Weybourne mill, while a few protected the railway.[1]

Weybourne and Mundesley were each fortified with six 60-pounder guns, manned by the Royal Field Artillery. There were two 4.7-inch guns at Cromer, one at Gorleston, and 15-pounders were emplaced at Eccles, Newport and Caister-on-Sea; Salthouse had two. These would have been of little use against enemy shipping, but could have been effective against disembarking troops. Finally an armoured train, one of only two provided nationwide, was stationed at North Walsham, perhaps more to reassure the public than to play any decisive military role, since it could have been put out of action by simply blowing up a section of the line.

In January 1916 the General Staff decided that the Germans were able to carry out more than mere nuisance raids, calculating that they might be able to land up to 160,000 men on the east coast, and that it could take the Royal Navy 24 to 28 hours to arrive on the spot. The General Staff considered such an attack unlikely, but thought that precautions should be taken.[2] Astonishingly the War Cabinet decided to take the risk of limiting Home Defence forces in the area from the Wash to Selsey Bill to only as many 'as would deter an enemy force of up to 30,000 men attempting a

landing'.[3] After the indecisive Battle of Jutland, fears of a large-scale raid designed to attack London increased. Inland defences were planned in addition to these coastal fortifications, though the aim was to prevent the enemy from getting off the beaches at all.

In Norfolk a line of defences was constructed along the course of the River Ant. The line began at the coast, at Stiffkey, ran along to Weybourne, and then through Beeston Regis, Aylmerton, Hanworth and Gunton until it joined the Ant at Bradfield. Almost all the river crossings down to Wayford Bridge were fortified with one or more pillboxes, and probably also with trenches which have since disappeared. These pillboxes seem usually to have been built in pairs, for mutual support. The River Ant was used again as a stop line in the Second World War, and more modern defences are frequently seen alongside the First World War pillboxes. An unusual case of a First World War pillbox being used in the Second World War may be found at West Runton, where a Second World War skin has been added to a First World War pillbox to strengthen it.[4]

Three different types of pillboxes were constructed in Norfolk. The first was a small emplacement built of poured concrete with an overhanging roof, similar in appearance to its namesake at the chemist's. Only one of these is known still to exist in Norfolk, on the north bank of Breydon Water, near Great Yarmouth.[5] It has now been buried by dredging work.

*A pair of hexagonal First World War pillboxes built either side of the A47, the road which an invading force would have used to get inland from Great Yarmouth.*[6] *Only three examples of this type of pillbox survive in Norfolk. (1998)*

← →

The second type was a larger circular pillbox, made of concrete blocks. Like the third type, it was equipped with the additional refinements of ventilation holes in the roof, of thick steel doors which could be locked on either side, and of metal shutters covering the loopholes, to be raised as necessary. The loopholes were often placed on different levels. Several examples of this design may still be found at the crossings of the River Ant.

The third type of pillbox was hexagonal and made of poured concrete. It appears much more similar to the common Second World War design than the others. An example at St Olaves Bridge, at Haddiscoe,[7] well-known because of the hexagonal boatyard office built on its roof in the 1960s, has a plate on the side of it reading 'St. Olaves Hall', a piece of First World War humour. Sadly the plate was painted over a few years ago, rendering the writing illegible. On the inside of one of the doors is the number 37, possibly indicating the number of pillboxes constructed in Norfolk; at least 30 are known to have been built.

Occasionally the pillbox designs would be modified as was thought suitable for the site. Neither of the pillboxes at Spa Common,[8] near North Walsham, conforms perfectly to a standard design. Although both are based on the second type described above, one is kidney-shaped, and the other is raised up, with steps leading to the entrance.

The defence system was still being enlarged as late as 1918, as indicated by writing scratched into the concrete on a pillbox at Sea Palling.[9]

*An example of the concrete block design of pillbox at Bacton* [10] *(1998)*

*The interior of a hexagonal pillbox near Great Yarmouth, showing the poured concrete construction and the differing heights of the loopholes - a feature often found on First World War pillboxes. The sliding steel shutters over the loopholes have been removed. (1998)*

At the end of the War the batteries were dismantled, the trenches filled in and the barbed wire removed. The pillboxes are the only reminder of this period of defence building, and only some of those have survived.

*First World War graffiti scratched into the concrete on a pillbox at Sea Palling, showing that it was built by men of the Royal Engineers in July 1918 (1997)*

**Notes to The Great War**

[1] Maps in the archives of the Walpole family at Wolterton Hall: 10/49.
[2] PRO: WO 33/771.
[3] PRO: WO 33/892.
[4] TG 1795 4298.
[5] TG 4909 0742.
[6] TG 5049 0921 and TG 5053 0889.
[7] TM 4559 9932
[8] TG 3001 3060 and TG 2994 3069
[9] TG 4218 2691.
[10] TG 3390 3360.

## FIRST AND SECOND WORLD WAR COASTAL DEFENCES

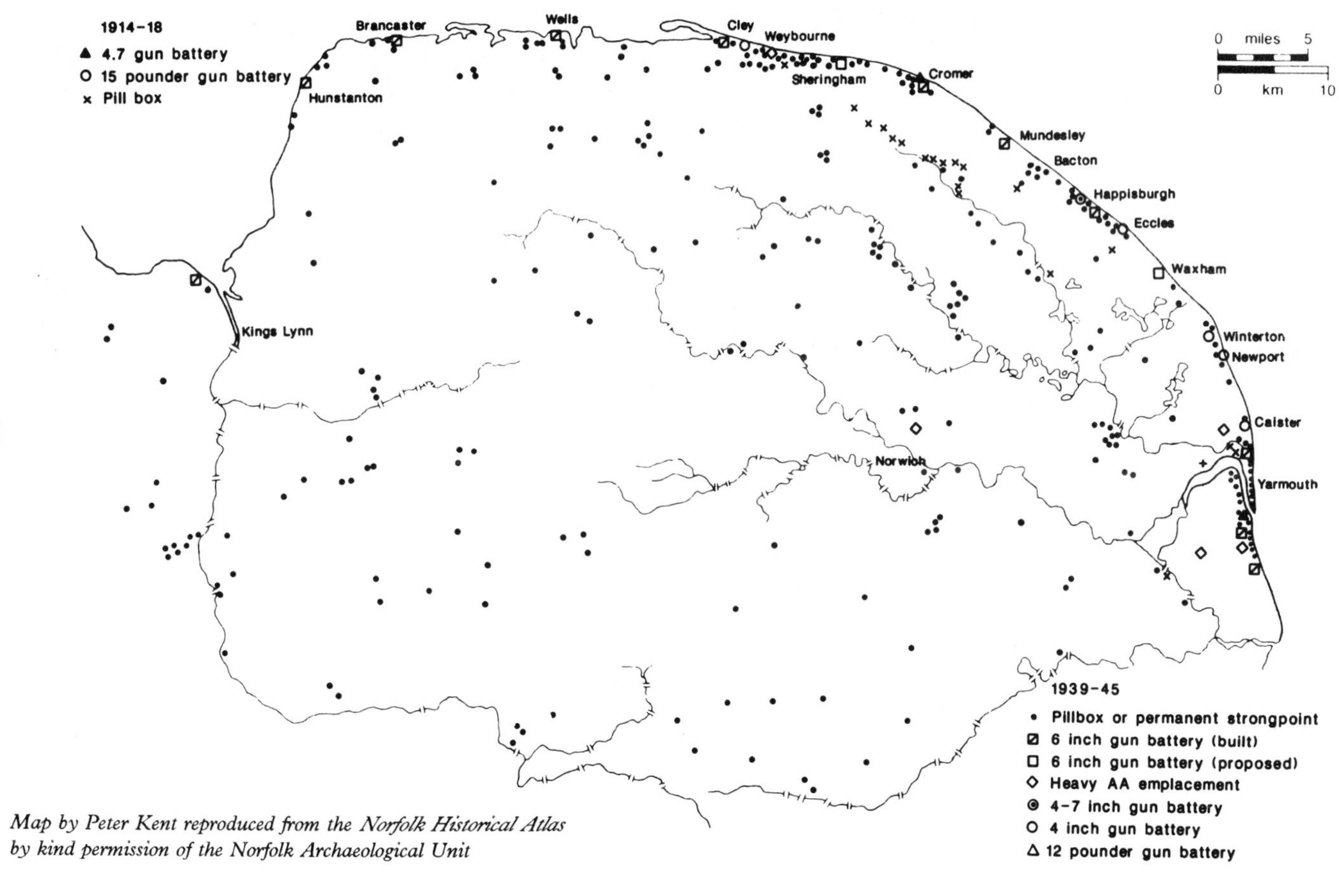


*Map by Peter Kent reproduced from the Norfolk Historical Atlas by kind permission of the Norfolk Archaeological Unit*

# THE SECOND WORLD WAR

## The coastal crust

The threat posed by the Germans after the fall of France in June 1940 was of a much more alarming scale than that of previous invasion scares. With Norway occupied in addition to France and the Low Countries, a very large section of Britain's coast was potentially at risk. The only solution was to defend every part of the coast where troops could feasibly be disembarked. Reconnaissance was carried out in May and June 1940 to assess Norfolk's vulnerability to landings by enemy tanks, infantry and aircraft. It was feared that the Germans had already done similar research: before the war a German cable ship had been observed just off the coast at Weybourne.[1] The North Norfolk coast is prone to rapid alteration of weather conditions. According to the British Admiral Dreyer, 'A complete change can occur in under an hour without warning, even in summer months'.[2] He concluded that anyone landing tanks there would probably have local knowledge, and that the Norwich Command must 'be prepared for an infantry attack on any portion of the coast'.[3]

*Anti-tank blocks at Winterton.[4] The names of the men who built them can be seen on the nearest block, written in the concrete as it was drying. The line on the right was built some months later, replacing the blocks on the left, which had sunk so low into the dunes as to become ineffective. (1998)*

Reconnaissance in May identified the areas suitable for the landing of tanks as King's Lynn, Heacham, Blakeney to Sheringham, and Bacton Green to Winterton Ness.[5] According to a report of 14th June by Admiral Dreyer, however, the conclusions had been reached on the wrong assumptions, owing to an insufficient knowledge of the conditions necessary for the disembarkation of tanks. From Cley to Sheringham, where there was 'an excellent landing beach',[6] the area between the beach and the coast road had been flooded, but Dreyer considered this measure ineffective.

Much of the coastal area was marshy and had large inland stretches of water, which would restrict enemy vehicles to the roads. But these would not prove obstacles to infantry, and the expanses of water were ideal for the landing of enemy aircraft, as were some of the beaches at low water. Gaps in the cliffs or dunes were to be blocked with concrete obstacles, mines and wire. Piers and harbours could offer facilities for landing stores and personnel. In July 1940 a gap was blown in Cromer pier, which then had to be bridged in order to provide access to the lifeboat stranded at the end of it![7]

The Wash was considered particularly vulnerable. 'Without indulging in "the painting of pictures"', Admiral Dreyer's report states, 'it is not unreasonable to consider the case of the enemy landing on the beach north of Skegness and simultaneously on the Southwold beaches and rushing the Wash with large bodies of troops in fast motor boats landing at King's Lynn and Boston [in Lincolnshire] and opening the Boston sluices to flood the country in a southerly direction thus impeding lateral movement by the defenders. The situation to be still further complicated by a diversionary landing well to the northward.'[8] The navigation marks in the channels were removed, though this would have achieved little, as ships with draughts of less than fifteen feet could still navigate anywhere over the Wash at high water. In addition Dreyer recommended laying a minefield. The idea of inundating coastal areas to hinder the enemy had been considered, but with one or two exceptions had been rejected. The Commander-in-Chief (C-in-C) of the Home Forces thought it would harm the nation's food supply more than anything else, besides offering the enemy large open stretches of water on which to land aircraft.[9]

## Defending the beaches

Norfolk's popular coastline, traditionally offering miles of golden sand to the holidaymaker, became scarred with a myriad of obstacles and defences. The beaches were choked with anti-tank blocks, backed up by endless coils of barbed wire and mines by the thousand. Metal scaffolding was erected in the sea itself in an attempt to prevent flat-bottomed barges reaching the shore. As an additional hindrance the scaffolding was laced with mines.

*Beach defences still in place at Bacton in 1947, the anti-boat scaffolding clearly visible. A rather unusual spot for a picnic! (Cecil Perham)*

The anti-boat scaffolding was not particularly effective, however. A test carried out in December 1941 showed that the detonation of one of the mines caused sufficient damage for a boat up to fifteen feet wide to be able to break through, and that the blast might disable other mines nearby.[10]

Vulnerable areas were further protected with trenches and pillboxes. Weybourne Hope, for example, was heavily defended. The archaeological evidence of the derelict remains on the beach combined with Ordnance Survey photographs of 1954 suggests that there were four machine-gun emplacements and an anti-tank pillbox in the space of around fifty yards. In addition to this there were heavy concentrations of pillboxes just inland; in the Weybourne area alone there were at least 34 pillboxes, though some of these were built to protect the anti-aircraft camp.

*A heavy machine-gun pillbox at Weybourne Hope.*[11] *The loophole is staircased, to stop enemy bullets entering the strongpoint. In the background another pillbox can be seen, one of several in this area. (1997)*

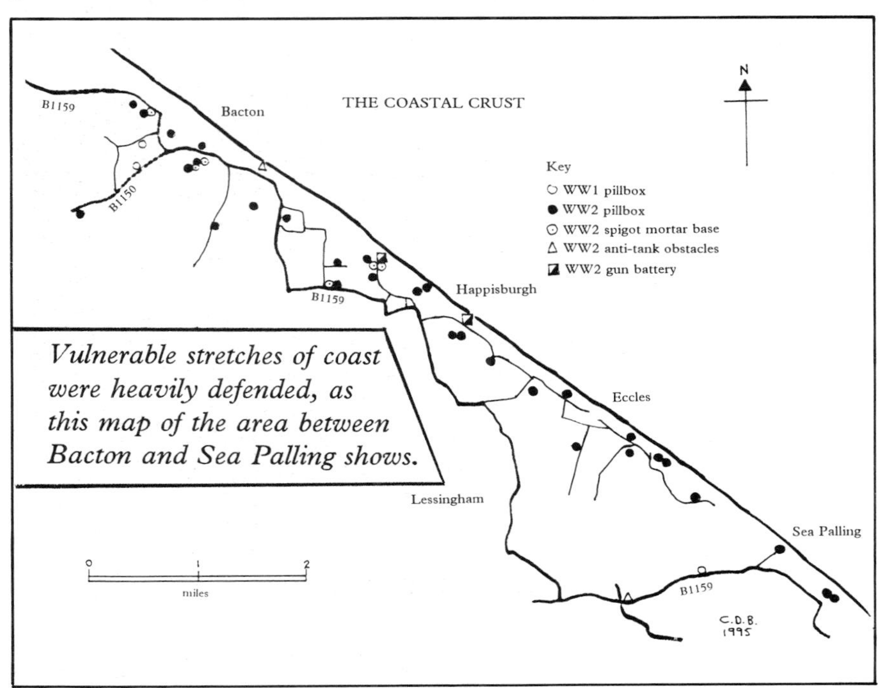


*Vulnerable stretches of coast were heavily defended, as this map of the area between Bacton and Sea Palling shows.*

Great Yarmouth was turned into a fortress, with a line of pillboxes, road blocks and trenches surrounding it on the landward side. A pillbox remains at the junction of two inland defence lines, the River Bure and River Yare.[12]

*Two 1940 photographs showing a type 22 pillbox at Great Yarmouth, backed up by trenches (in the first picture another pillbox can be seen in the background, on the left). A practice assault is under way, involving the 4th Norfolk Regiment. Natural camouflage has been used on the roof of the pillbox. (Mr Puttnam)*[13]

By 4th June 1940 all reconnaissance of the beaches was complete in Eastern Command. Work had begun on pillboxes and wire defences on the beaches. Contracts had been placed for concrete anti-tank obstacles. Nationwide, 50,000 anti-tank mines had been issued and orders placed for a further 200,000. Work was in progress to block almost all landing-grounds within five miles of selected ports from Great Yarmouth in Norfolk to Newhaven in Sussex. Preparations for the demolition of the bridges on the roads leading inland from the ports were nearly complete.

*The view through one of the loopholes of a pillbox at Cromer*[14] *(1998)*

It was estimated that within one week all 6-inch batteries would be complete. Sites for batteries with smaller guns were being reconnoitered. Wires were being stretched across wide roads to prevent enemy aircraft landing on them. But despite all the anti-tank emplacements being constructed around the country only 120 six-pounder guns and fewer than 200 two-pounder guns, both for use against tanks, were available nationwide.[15]

## Gun batteries

The installation of artillery guns was a major priority. There had been virtually no planning of fortifications between the wars, and makeshift batteries had to be designed very quickly. Most were armed with two 6-inch guns which had been removed from ships in the 1920s. The *Manual of Coast Defence, 1939* stated that 'The

6-inch gun on a 15° mounting may be considered the standard defence against vessels lighter than cruisers, and is the principal close defence weapon'. It was capable of firing eight rounds per minute.[16] These guns were not in perfect condition, nor was ammunition in plentiful supply, so the value of these 'emergency batteries' is debatable. Cromer battery's guns, for instance, dated from 1906 and 1912, and had been stripped from HMS *Africa* and HMS *Dublin*.[17]

*A casemate for a 4.7-inch gun at Happisburgh battery [18] (1998)*

The guns were mounted in brick and concrete casemates, well suited to batteries which had to be thrown together quickly, since they could be built around any type of mounting. Magazines and shelters were built between the casemates, half-buried for extra

*Removing camouflage nets from one of two 6-inch guns at North Denes Battery, Great Yarmouth, manned by the 325th Coast Battery, 514th Coast Regiment AA 2nd Corps*

*Placing charges on a trolley in the buried magazines. They will then be carried by hand up to the gun platforms. (Mr Puttnam, 1941)*[19]

protection. The complex was commanded from the battery observation post, a tall building in the centre of the battery.

Emergency batteries were built at King's Lynn, Hunstanton, Brancaster, Wells, Cley-next-the-Sea, Sheringham, Cromer, Mundesley, Happisburgh, Winterton and Great Yarmouth - where there were three. All were armed with two 6-inch naval guns except Winterton, which had 4-inch guns, and the Gorleston Pier battery, which had 12-pounder quick-firing guns. Although never used in action, the batteries did not survive the war without damage. Happisburgh battery collapsed on to the beach shortly after being built, and was rebuilt with 4.7-inch guns at a new site slightly to the north of the village. In early 1941 the Gorleston Pier battery was damaged when a British torpedo head accidentally exploded under the pier, and one of the guns and a searchlight had to be moved to a site north of the harbour.[20]

The batteries were well defended, as the plan of the one at Winterton shows. In addition to two perimeters of barbed wire, there

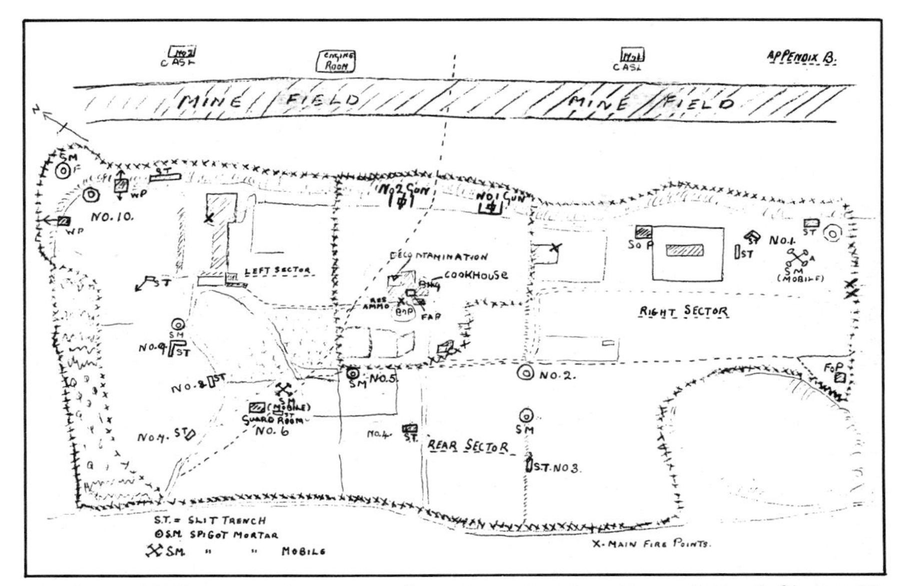


*A plan of Winterton battery, taken from its Fort Record Book.[21] CASL stands for coastal artillery searchlight, WP for weapon pit.*

were three pillboxes and several spigot mortars, slit trenches and weapon pits. Full provision had to be made for the garrison, so there was an officers' mess, a sergeants' mess, a fitter's shop, an assault course and even a greenhouse amongst other facilities, all within the outer perimeter. The battery observation post (BOP) was a converted lighthouse, which had been disused since 1921. The map was probably made by the Home Guard, who were put in charge of the battery around 1943. The spigot mortar was a Home Guard weapon, and it was the Norfolk Home Guard that invented the 'Atkins' Mobile Mounting for this weapon, marked on the map.[22] After the war, the site was converted into the Hotel Hermanus, and several of the original buildings survive, converted for peacetime use.[23]

Arcs of fire could be crossed by neighbouring batteries, and extra firepower came from inland batteries. Five batteries of 28-pounders, 25-pounders, 18-pounders and 9.2-inch howitzers were positioned near Holt to give support to the coastal batteries at Wells, Cley and

*Winterton battery today. The lighthouse was used as the observation post; the building on the left was the canteen. The concrete platform in the foreground is a ventilation point for the underground magazines. (1998)*

Sheringham, and additional 18-pounder naval guns were sited at Weybourne. In January 1941 the 147th Field Regiment Royal Artillery moved to Norfolk, and Captain P.W.Gee recalls further details of the batteries:

> Regimental H.Q. was at Holt and gun positions were at Salthouse Heath, Warren House [in High Kelling, near Weybourne], Sheringham Hall, Aylmerton and Cromer. Muckleburgh Hill between Sheringham and Cromer was a fine point of observation and during the summer many artillery demonstrations were staged for visiting Commanders and the Press without loss of life, material or reputation. Communication between Muckleburgh Hill and the guns was long and sometimes unreliable. On the occasion of a demonstration of unusual importance communication both by wireless and telephone line was non-existent; Major J.M.Redmayne, with that aptitude for improvisation of which he was master, wrote firing orders on the back of a cigarette packet and sent it to the guns by despatch rider. The concentration of shells fell into the sea at the appointed time and in the appointed place.[24]

In November 1945 the Coast Artillery Investigation Committee reported on the types of battery built during the Second World War.[25] The nature of the emergency batteries had resulted in their being poorly designed; the Committee noted that 'Many local designs of emplacements and shields were provided which were inadequate to protect the gun from the effects of air bombardment, and demonstrated the need for provision of standard designs to suit a strictly limited number of "standard" situations'.

*The gun platforms of the 6-inch battery at Mundesley, the best preserved of the Norfolk batteries.[26] The overhead protection for the guns has been removed. (1998)*

The casemate mounting was considered obsolete. Amongst other disadvantages, it provided a limited field of fire, it tended to offer insufficient protection for the gun, and it was a large and conspicuous target. The designs recommended by the Committee featured turret mountings, with the shell stores, engine room, plotting room, accommodation and all the other facilities needed by the battery housed in an enormous underground concrete complex built beneath the turret. A great deal of concrete was to be used to provide sufficient protection, but it was felt that the expense was justified: 'one properly constructed battery is worth any number of ill-conceived makeshifts' - a very damning comment on the emergency batteries.[27]

## Inland defences

Today pillboxes usually seem scattered and isolated. This, however, is largely the result of demolition. Airfields, radar stations, searchlight installations and such establishments had their own pillboxes for protection, but the other inland defences were carefully arranged according to a general defence system.

Britain had a series of defence lines, the most important of which was the GHQ line, built to protect London and the industrial Midlands. Norfolk had its own stop lines, which fitted into this larger defence system. These were designed merely to slow the enemy down; hence the successive lines of defence, unlike the principle behind the Maginot Line.

Norfolk's lines were based on the courses of the Rivers Ant, Bure, Wensum, Yare and Ouse. The rivers were deep enough to prevent tanks fording them, and were treated as natural anti-tank ditches, as were railway cuttings in some parts of the country. The crossings of the rivers were defended with anti-tank obstacles and pillboxes, and the bridges were mined. The North Walsham and Dilham Canal, which had extended the length of the navigable Ant by eight miles, had been disused since 1935, and had to be deepened and widened to form a sufficient obstacle.[28] Today the canal has become choked above Honing Lock, and it is difficult to imagine that such a tiny trickle could have held up a tank. On the Bure, defences remain at every bridge from Ingworth to Acle, except at Wroxham, where a pillbox[29] has been removed.

The map opposite shows the defences of Thursford, a small village near Fakenham, in the Second World War. Thursford is by the junction of the B1354 with the A148, and is close to a railway (closed in 1959). All the roads leading to the junction are blocked by anti-tank rails, which could quickly be fitted into sockets in the road surface. All the approaches to the road junction are within

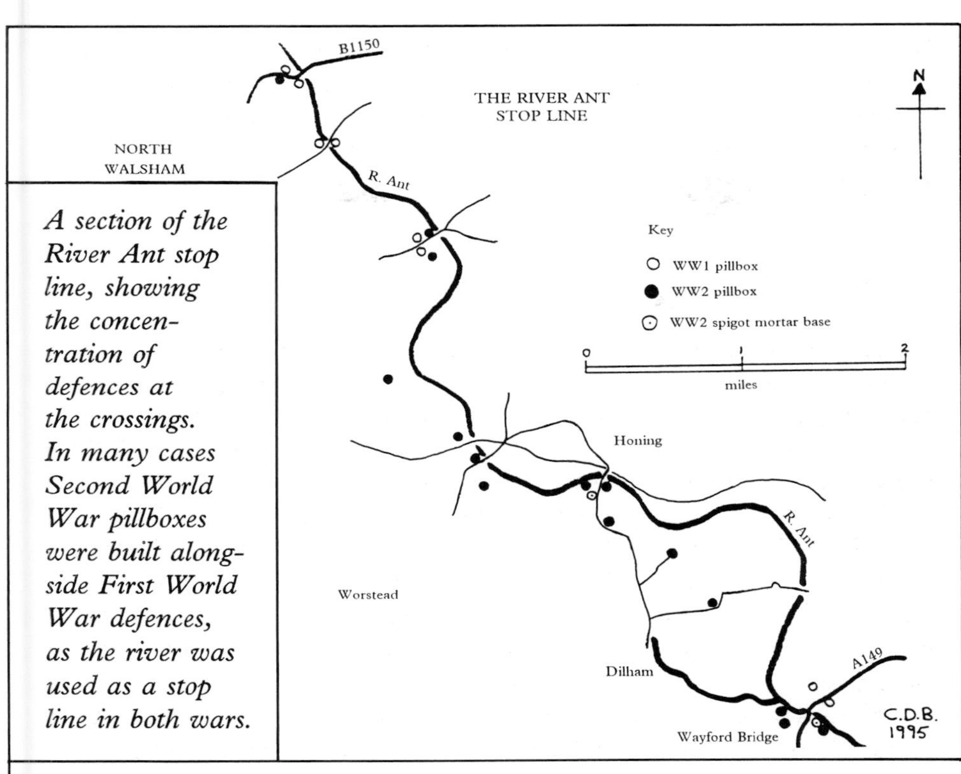


*A section of the River Ant stop line, showing the concentration of defences at the crossings. In many cases Second World War pillboxes were built alongside First World War defences, as the river was used as a stop line in both wars.*

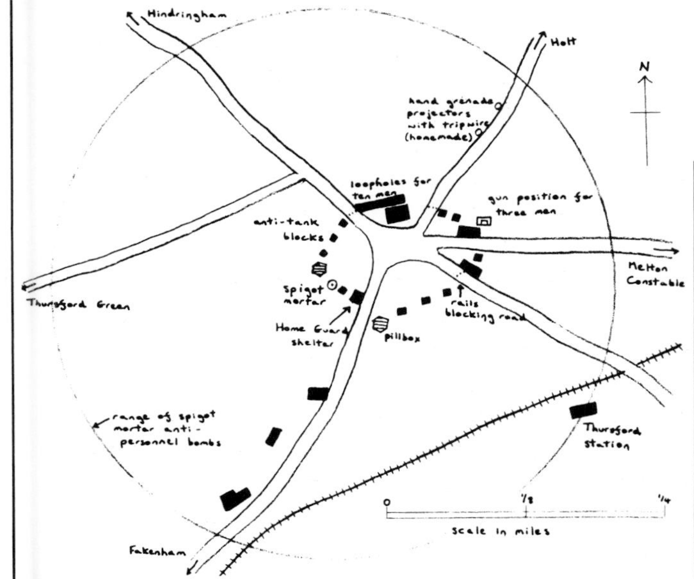


*The Second World War defences at Thursford, - based on a map drawn in 1995 by Mr D. Bailey, a former member of the Thursford Home Guard*

range of the spigot mortar. These defences were manned by thirty men from the Home Guard of Thursford and Barney, a neighbouring village. Of all the defences shown, only one pillbox, the Home Guard shelter and the loopholes (now blocked up) cut into the wall behind the Crawfish public house survive today.

## Pillboxes

'Experience in the Polish Campaign has shown that direct attack against pillboxes cannot succeed', it was stated in the Oslo Report, a document concerning scientific developments in Germany which came into British hands in November 1939.[30] The crews had to be overcome with gas shells and flame-throwers. Pillboxes were by far the most common form of defence built in Britain, and despite post-war demolition of these 'eyesores' hundreds of them still survive in Norfolk. Various types were built, designed for different situations. The standard versions, designed by FW3, a branch of Fortifications and Works at the War Office, were:

Type 22:[31] small hexagonal pillbox for six men, with five light machine-guns (LMGs) and one rifle.

Type 23: small rectangular pillbox with two chambers, one roofed and one open, for a light anti-aircraft (AA) weapon; for four men, with three LMGs and one rifle.

Type 24: large hexagonal pillbox with thick walls and a long entrance side, for eight men with five LMGs and two rifles.[32]

Type 25: small circular pillbox for four men with three LMGs or rifles.

Type 26: small square pillbox for five men with four LMGs.

Type 27: large hexagonal or octagonal pillbox, with an open chamber in the middle for a light AA weapon, for ten men. No octagonal examples are known in Norfolk.

Type 28: large rectangular or square pillbox for a 2- or 6-pounder anti-tank gun. There are various different versions of this design, but the most common consisted of two chambers, for ten men with three LMGs and a 2-pounder gun (type 28A).

Heavy Machine-Gun (HMG) pillbox or emplacement: thick-walled square pillbox, for four men with two rifles and an HMG. A commonly found Norfolk variant consists of a pair of emplacements joined together at an angle of 120° enabling the guns to sweep along a beach.[33]

*A type 22 pillbox at Happisburgh with staircased loopholes, designed to prevent splinters being deflected into the pillbox.[34] The entrance was originally built on the left, so that the pillbox would face out to sea, and then sealed up and rebuilt on the seaward side, as the pillbox was designed to defend Happisburgh battery from an attack from the landward side. On the roof are the remains of a Royal Observer Corps post built in 1958. (1998)*

The designs caused some complaints. The Chief Engineer of the Home Forces received many criticisms that the loopholes were being constructed at too great a height to enable most men to shoot through them![35] Even the Bishop of Truro wrote to the War Office, concerned that the standard design of loophole, with sloped sides in the outside, offered insufficient protection to the men inside the pillbox, and suggesting an alternative design.[36]

There was sometimes provision for extra weapons to be mounted in or on pillboxes. A few pillboxes have small loopholes at ground level in addition to the main LMG loopholes, for the use of anti-tank rifles.[37] Anti-aircraft mountings are very occasionally found on the roofs, usually in the form of a metal cone designed for an Oerlikon gun. A wall of either bricks or sandbags would enable the crew to take cover from machine-gun fire.

*A mounting for an Oerlikon anti-aircraft gun on the roof of a type 22 pillbox at Mundesley.[38] The wall, probably made higher with sandbags, was designed to offer some degree of protection to the crew. (1998)*

Types 23 and 27 were specifically designed for use against both infantry and aircraft, and each feature an open chamber in which a machine-gun could be mounted on a wooden post. A pillbox at Cley-next-the-Sea still has a concrete cover over the anti-aircraft chamber for use when the room was not needed.[39]

As protection against enemy bullets entering a pillbox and ricocheting round inside, thus killing all the defenders, 'baffle' walls were built in the larger pillboxes. These were usually Y-shaped in cross-section, the top part of the 'Y' being nearest the entrance. An internal wall was not always practical, however, as in the case of the machine-gun pillbox, which had a large concrete table inside to support the HMG tripod. In such cases, blast walls were often built outside the entrance. Some loopholes were staircased, to prevent splinters from bullets shattering against the concrete being projected into the pillbox, as was possible with the standard sloped design.

A shutter was designed which could be fitted over the loopholes as protection against flame-throwers. But a version tested was found to be ineffective.[40] The problem was further complicated by the necessity of making several different designs, to fit around the different types of mounting found on various pillboxes. The Turnbull mountings usually found on type 24s presented particular problems.[41]

Most First World War pillboxes had thick steel doors, but this was very unusual on their Second World War descendants. Some, in particular type 24s and a few 22s, had skeletal doors, which would have been of little use in combat, and were more likely designed rather to keep meddlesome children out. These are very occasionally found still in situ today. They seem, however, to have been more trouble than they were worth. One evening two members of the Home Guard went to check on a pillbox on Horstead Common[42] only to be locked in when the door jammed. They were unable to open it from inside, and, since no one could hear their shouting, they were forced to spend the night in the pillbox. By the next morning, a Sunday, they were growing desperate, and seeing the villagers going to the nearby church, they fired their guns in their direction to attract their attention! Miraculously no one rang the church bells, and the weary men were let out.[43] A more serious invasion alert, which turned out to be a false alarm, occurred on 7th September 1940. Eastern and Southern Commands were given warning of imminent invasion (the 'Cromwell' order), and several bridges were blown up in preparation for the arrival of the Germans, expected within the next twelve hours.[44]

A report comparing the merits of concrete and earthworks concluded that 'Standardized specifications covering the general structure of both earth and concrete works and of particular features such as fire steps or embrasures, are essential, but they must be capable of the necessary adaptation to the ground, houses, cliffs,

*Pillboxes were not necessarily as comfortless for their Second World War garrisons as they appear today. These members of the Royal Artillery appear quite at home in this type 28 pillbox near Chelmsford. A 6-pounder anti-tank gun, probably stripped from a First World War 'male' tank, fills the loophole. A set of spanners for the gun can be seen on the left. (Mr Puttnam, 1940)* [45]

etc'.[46] A number of pillboxes may be found with modifications to the standard designs, and since these are often regional it may have been the result of the opinions of the individual officers in charge of construction. Several examples of a variant of the type 26 design may be found at Weybourne.[47] These have the loopholes placed to one end of each side to make room for an internal wall. A few pillboxes, such as the heavy machine-gun pillbox at Oulton Airfield,[48] are unique. Indeed there is so much variation between pillboxes even of the same type that Mike Osborne, author of the article 'Pillbox Typology',[49] has concluded that no two were exactly alike.

The Air Ministry had designs of their own. While it was considered that principally earthworks should be used for the defence of airfields, pillboxes were desirable for the protection they offered, and because airfield defences were likely to be of a more permanent nature.[50] But there was much disagreement about the usefulness of pillboxes in protecting airfields. The C-in-C, Southern Command, wrote 'I do not encourage the garrisons of aerodromes to fight from pillboxes; my policy is to adopt the locality system of trenches which are easier to conceal and easier to fight from'.[51] Eastern Command's opinion, however, was that pillboxes were 'useful on certain aerodromes'.[52]

In addition to the standard types, eight main Air Ministry designs have been identified in Norfolk, bearing no discernible relation to the main types. These appear to have been built in very small numbers, as so few have been located. Often an airfield seems to have a design exclusive to that place, as with the small pillboxes at West Raynham Airfield. Some airfields had Battle Headquarters, underground bomb-proof buildings with an observation room jutting up above the ground. From this building the Station Commander could direct the defence of the airfield. A few examples survive in Norfolk.[53] West Beckham and Stoke Holy Cross radar stations each have types of pillboxes believed to be unique to those locations, in addition to standard 22s.

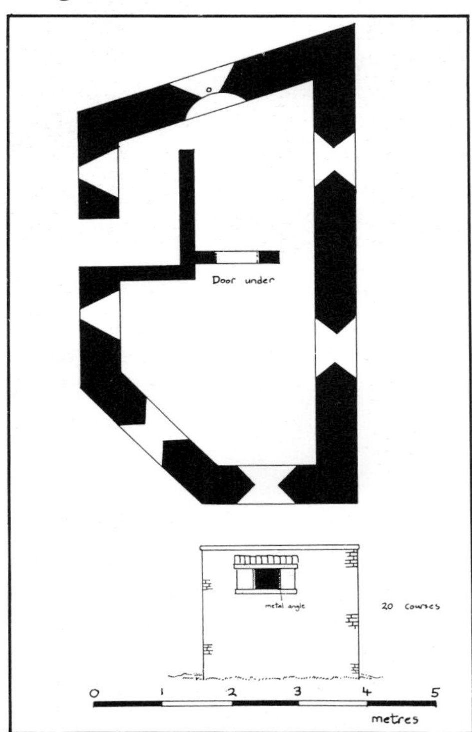


*An Air Ministry design employed at Coltishall Airfield.[54] This, and many other Air Ministry designs, illustrate why there was concern about the degree of protection offered to the garrison: they were what the Chief Engineer, Home Forces, called 'the "sieve" type of pillbox...nothing but a death trap'. (Drawing by Peter Kent)*

As late as August 1941 new types of pillbox designed for airfields were being considered, one of them pentagonal. Both are strikingly different from earlier designs, with only two loopholes and living accommodation for two men provided. Alternative layouts were provided as well, with the loopholes in different positions to suit different sites.[55] These were never built.[56]

## Unusual pillboxes

In addition to these standard types, there were special types of pillboxes designed for specific purposes.

The Alan Williams Turret was a small steel turret, which could rotate, giving an all-round field of fire. Designed for two men, it could also be used in an anti-aircraft role. This was considered a desirable alternative to a conventional pillbox as it was lower and could be easily concealed. However it was not strong enough to withstand armour-piercing small arms ammunition or shells fired from a 2-pounder gun.

*An Alan Williams Turret with a Lewis gun mounted for use against aircraft. The loophole facing the camera was for use against infantry. The shutters for this loophole, and the hatches for the entrance and the anti-aircraft opening, are often missing from turrets found today, making them look more dangerous for their crews than they actually were. This example is at Swansea. (Lieutenant Taylor, 1941)*[57]

The C-in-C, Southern Command, commented that 'As a turret for A.A. use this type has no value, it is far too difficult to traverse and the field of fire is too small for A.A. work'.[58] He recommended it only for ground defence of beaches or aerodromes, used in conjunction with trenches. An example at Cromer, now demolished, had been built into the roof of a pillbox.[59] Another example at Cley-next-the-Sea [60] is pictured on the cover of this book.

The Pickett Hamilton Fort or Disappearing Pillbox was a highly ingenious design for use on airfields. It could sink into the ground on a counterbalance or a hydraulic mechanism in a few seconds so that it would not be an obstacle to aeroplanes. They were usually built in threes, and could be placed very close to the main runways. It was even suggested that they be built on the slopes of humpback bridges, where the enemy vehicle would be unable to get its gun low enough to fire back.[61] They took eight days to build and test, and cost around £230-£250.

The C-in-C, Southern Command, however, was sceptical:

> At present all forms of the Pickett Hamilton Fort which have been erected in this Command are liable to jam. Those which are raised by means of compressed air are definitely dangerous and should be abandoned. There appears to be considerable tactical difficulty in deciding when to put the crew in. In the event of surprise the crew would never get in in time and, since most attacks on aerodromes will come as a surprise, the value for these forts for aerodromes is doubtful.[62]

Eastern Command received an unusual objection to the design from the Commander of 4 Corps: 'I feel sure that it would have a pernicious psychological influence on the garrison who, in the event of an attack, would be greatly tempted to "close down" instead of carrying out their duty.'[63] Pickett Hamilton Forts still remain at Swanton Morley[64] and Norwich Airport.[65] When I was given permission to examine one of the Norwich Forts in 1992 it still had its hydraulic mechanism intact and apparently in very good condition.

The Norcon pillbox was a dreadfully perilous design, its sole advantage being its speed of construction. It consisted of a concrete pipe, pierced with several loopholes. They could be turned out at a

*A Pickett Hamilton Fort still remaining at Norwich Airport (originally Horsham St Faith Airfield), its hydraulic mechanism intact.*[66] *Here shown in the 'down' position, it would have presented no obstacle to taxiing aircraft. This was one of three built at the airfield. (1992)*

rate of around 20 per day, becoming bulletproof after 24 hours.[67] In its finished form it had a roof made of timber, corrugated iron and earth, and had the dubious additional protection of sandbags placed around the outside. (A similar design was made by Armco.[68]) After inspecting this type of pillbox in June 1940, the C-in-C, Home Forces, wanted them to be provided for aerodromes, mounted on lorries 'purchased from the scrap heap, their only qualification being that they should be able to travel 800 yards out into the aerodrome'.[69] Perhaps not surprisingly few appear to have been built; only three

*The Norcon pillbox, simply a concrete pipe. The large number of loopholes, when there was no baffle wall, presented a serious danger to the crew. Originally it would have had a simple roof and a surrounding of sandbags. This rare example is at Weybourne.*[70] *(1990)*

are known still to exist in Norfolk. Absurd as a type such as the Norcon may seem, similar pillboxes are still built today to protect airfields and radar stations.

Infantry section posts, L-shaped pillboxes with five loopholes on each side facing outwards, are occasionally found by the coast.

*The interior of an L-shaped section post at Cromer*[71] *(1998)*

Particularly bizarre, and probably unique, were the pillboxes built in the grounds of the Royal Naval Hospital, Great Yarmouth. These were in fact air raid shelters with loopholes added, thus reducing the protection offered to the occupants, since the loopholes would not keep out splinters and shrapnel. They were demolished in 1996.[72] Despite the possible danger, the War Office received requests for the public to be allowed to use pillboxes as air raid shelters, and they gave permission for certain pillboxes to be used for this purpose.[73]

Pillbox design quickly changed. In October 1941 the Chief Engineer of the Home Forces decided that the side of the pillbox facing the enemy was to be increased to a thickness of 6 feet and to have no loophole, with other pillboxes or earthworks covering one another. Other walls were to have concrete added below loophole level to increase their thickness to 3 feet 6 inches. Roofs were increased to a thickness of at least 1 foot 6 inches. 'In general, opportunity should be taken to eliminate many of the redundant loopholes with which the earlier type of pillboxes were "riddled". What may be called the "sieve" type of pillbox is nothing but a death trap.'[74] As a further safety measure, the arcs of fire from loopholes were not to exceed 40°.

In early 1941 Southern Command decided that 'Pillboxes have many disadvantages; they give a false sense of security to the garrison, make them static minded and prevent the full employment of their weapons'.[75] Finally on 25th February 1942 it was concluded that 'All experience of modern warfare points most strongly to the fact that the pillbox is not a suitable type of fortification for either coastal or nodal point [i.e. defensive inland strongpoint] defences'.[76]

## Camouflaging the defences

Pillboxes were difficult to conceal. A War Office report concluded that 'In most cases a choice will have to be made between the better protection afforded by concrete and the better concealment afforded by earthworks'.[77] They could be concealed by putting canvas screens in front of them, or by painting them. Since a pillbox could be given away by its harsh, straight outline, little wavy ridges were sometimes made on the roof to make it less conspicuous, as with a pillbox near Thetford.[78] Pillboxes are quite often found with earth camouflage on the roof, to disguise them from aerial reconnaisance. 'Cullecourt', wire netting covered with chicken feathers and camouflage paint, could also be used for this purpose.[79] An impressive use of natural camouflage can be seen at Weybourne Hope, where a machine-gun emplacement was built into the cliff, its large loophole visible to the enemy only from the beach.

*A heavy machine-gun pillbox, built into the cliff at Weybourne Hope.[80] It faces along the beach, covering the main exit, and so is invisible from the seaward side. (1998)*

Pillboxes were not always disguised as undergrowth; two Norfolk pillboxes, for instance, were convincingly disguised as a milk bar and a holiday chalet.[81]

*A type 27 pillbox disguised as a shed. Hatches fitted over the loopholes to conceal them are folded down in this picture, making the pillbox ready for action. The location of this pillbox is not known, though it is probably not in Norfolk. (Captain Console, 1941)*[82]

*The fortified outhouse extension to Acle Manor House, commanding what was then the main approach to Norwich from Great Yarmouth. One loophole is visible, in place of a window. (1996)*

The most effective way to camouflage a strongpoint was to build it into an existing structure. Norfolk has some excellent examples of this type of concealment, such as the pillbox built as an extension to Acle Manor House,[83] covering an important road junction. This took in even the estate agent, whose brochure described it, when the house was up for sale a few years ago, as 'believed to have been the original village lock-up'!

*Loopholes cut into the corner of a barn at Tunstall, near Great Yarmouth [84] (1998)*

Two windmills were converted into multi-storey pillboxes, the Stracey Arms,[85] and the drainage pump at Ludham Bridge.[86] The Stracey Arms provides a superb view across to Great Yarmouth and to Acle, where a ring of defences blocked the approach road from Yarmouth and from across the River Bure. Nearby is another camouflaged strongpoint, built into a barn at Tunstall. These drainage mills had not been built with the object of protecting their occupants, so the Stracey Arms had one of its entrances and some of its windows blocked up, while the mill at Ludham had a blast wall added to its doorway. Both pillboxes would have been serious dangers to their crews, as they had no internal walls but several loopholes. Two of the windows on one of the gun floors at Ludham Bridge were left completely unblocked. The loopholes at Ludham Bridge still remain, but the loopholes at the Stracey Arms were bricked up when the mill was restored in 1961.

*The Stracey Arms windmill, near Great Yarmouth, converted into a camouflaged multi-storey pillbox. (Harry Meyer, 1950, reproduced by courtesy of Arthur C. Smith)*

Another mill to play its part in the defence system was the derelict corn mill at Ingham, near Stalham, which had a Royal Observer Corps post built at the top of the tower, still there today.[87] It was reached by a long ladder bolted to the outside of the mill.

*The derelict drainage mill at Ludham Bridge, used as a two-storey pillbox. The wooden floor, now rotted away, did not permit the building of a baffle wall to protect the defenders. (1998)*

Most spectacular of all was a strongpoint built inside the ruins of Bromholme Priory at Bacton.[88] The remains made it possible to build a huge pillbox in the middle of a field without fear of its being spotted. The walls are solid concrete, thick enough to make the building shellproof. The size allowed the building of a large baffle wall inside. The four corner loopholes were for small arms, and the five other loopholes were for LMGs. This magnificent concealed pillbox was backed up by three spigot mortar bases, a loopholed wall and a pillbox concealed elsewhere in the Priory.

*The massive camouflaged pillbox in Bromholme Priory at Bacton*

*The entrance to the Bromholme Priory strongpoint. A small loophole may be seen either side of the entrance. (1998)*

## Anti-tank defences

A host of different designs of anti-tank obstacle was devised by the War Office. By far the most commonly-seen type is the large concrete cube, but pimples (also known rather more imaginatively as 'dragons' teeth'), tetrahedrons, buoys, cylinders, rails, ditches and walls were also built.

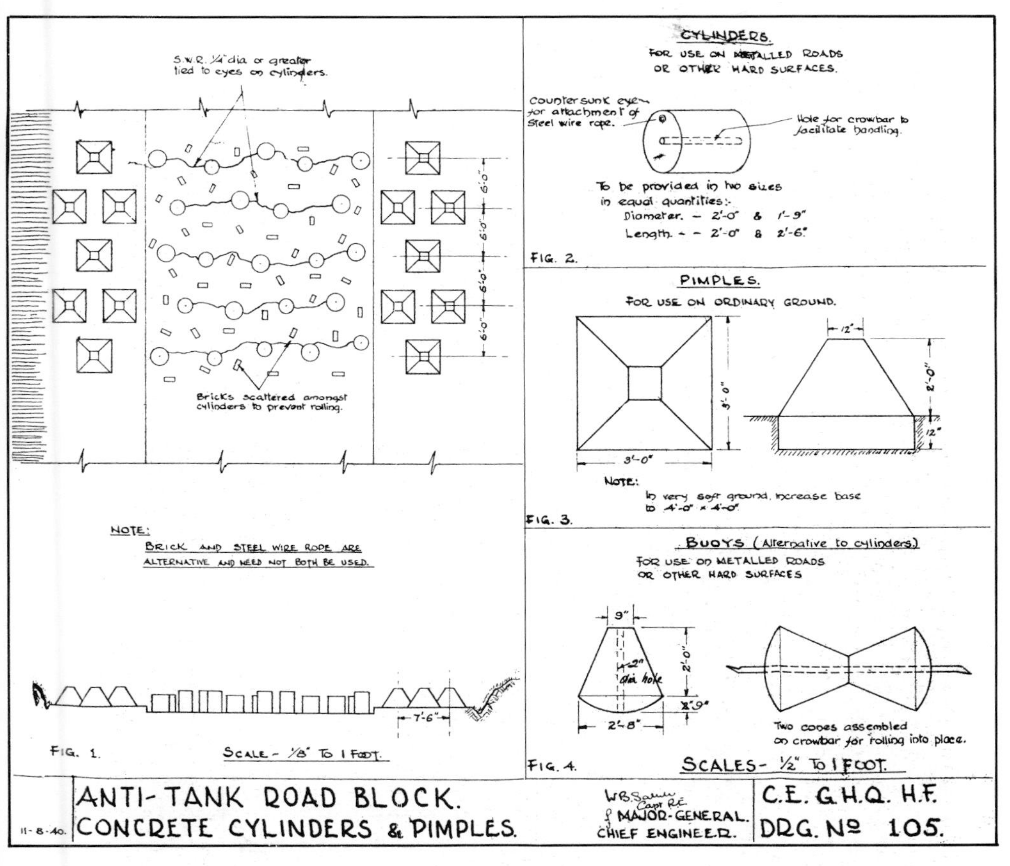


*A typical road block, consisting of anti-tank dragons' teeth (pimples) and cylinders, as prepared by the Chief Engineer, GHQ, Home Forces, 11th August 1940* [89]

Anti-tank blocks may often be found beside river crossings, usually accompanied by a pillbox. The blocks were sometimes designed to allow an obstacle to be stretched across the road between them, as at Heacham, where horizontal metal bars are fitted into slots in the sides of the blocks.[90] The blocks at Winterton (illustrated on page 11) bear the names of the men who built them, scratched in the concrete while it was drying.[91] The dates show that the two rows of blocks were built some months apart, probably because the first row had sunk into the sand. This would have rendered them useless, as a height of five feet above ground level was thought necessary to stop a tank.[92]

*A defended crossing of the River Bure at Burgh-next-Aylsham.[93] The blocks bar the approaches to the bridge, which would have been mined. (1998)*

*Vertical rails protruding from an anti-tank block beside the River Bure at Brampton, allowing a barricade to be stretched across the road.[94] This river crossing is also defended by a pillbox. (1996)*

Other kinds of concrete obstacle were sometimes improvised. Many of the blocks piled up at the foot of the cliff at Mundesley have been made by pouring concrete into oil drums.[95]

*Anti-tank blocks improvised by pouring concrete into oil drums on Mundesley beach. The brackets protruding from the top would have enabled the cylinders to be linked together. (1998)*

Anti-tank rails were designed to be concreted into sockets built in the road, with a tripwire stretched across the road between them. Anti-tank rails for the centre of the road would be cut, bent and drilled, and stored at the The rails at the sides of the road were installed at once, since they did not pose an obstacle to traffic. Very good examples survive at Narborough;[96] sockets beside the road can still be seen at Castle Rising.[97] Another type of obstacle involved stretching thick steel hawsers diagonally across the road, anchored at

*Roads had to be left clear for traffic until invasion was imminent. At this road block the anti-tank blocks have already been constructed (one of them is visible on the left), and men of the 6th Battalion, Norfolk Regiment are demonstrating how quickly rails can be fitted into sockets in the road to complete a barrier at Sheringham.[98] (Mr Puttnam, 1940)*

*Anti-tank rails blocking the crossings of the Middle Level Main Drain and Popham's Eau at the Three Holes Bridge, near Upwell.*[100] *They are overlooked by a type 28A pillbox, for a 2-pounder anti-tank gun, in the background. (Derek Manning, 1994)*

either end by concrete blocks.[99]

Tests were carried out on various different anti-tank obstacles in August 1940 with a 22½-ton 'I' tank. Many obstacles, such as buoys and rails, were found to be unsatisfactory, some of them being negotiated in less than a minute. Small obstacles did not form a sufficiently formidable barrier, while larger ones could be fired upon by the tank. However the tank was unable to get past the standard large concrete blocks. Natural obstacles such as ditches and scarped slopes were also found to be unsatisfactory, even against a light 18-ton Cruiser tank.

*An anti-tank ditch, covered by two pillboxes, bridging a gap in the cliffs near Weybourne.*[101] *A minefield was laid here as a further defence. (1999)*

The 'V' type of anti-tank ditch was found to be very effective against tanks of up to 25 tons. This consisted of a V-shaped trench 5 feet deep, preceded by a mound 5 feet 6 inches tall. The shape enabled two anti-tank guns to sweep along the trench, while the mound made it difficult to launch an assault bridge, used for crossing otherwise impassable obstacles, from the tank. Also this type of anti-tank ditch needed relatively little excavation, since the earth bank was dug out of the trench. However, the mound offered some protection to the enemy, so the bank would be flattened in places, but mined to prevent infantry crossing at these points.

A test was also carried out on a car filled with stones and supported on concrete blocks, and it was recommended that if it could be secured in some way, or a lorry used instead, this obstacle could be adequate and quick to construct.[102]

*Members of the Home Guard defending a road block at Swansea. This was part of a mock invasion in August 1941 also involving the Army, Navy, Air Force and ARP services. In practice these men would not have lasted long against the enemy, however effective the barricade might be. (Lieutenant Taylor)*[103]

None of these anti-tank defences was expected to be able to stop the enemy altogether. A report noted that 'All obstacles to wheeled or tracked vehicles have a delaying value only. The efficiency of the obstacle will determine the length of the delay but in order to exploit it, the obstacle must be covered by the fire of anti-tank and light automatic weapons.'[104]

## Other defences

Spigot mortar bases are often found covering roads, bridges, at gun batteries, or next to pillboxes. They are small cylindrical concrete mountings, given away by their shiny metal spikes, designed for the 29mm spigot mortar, or Blacker Bombard as it was also known. They seem usually to have been built two or three at a time. Given the large numbers of bases constructed, as opposed to the number of spigot mortars available, this was not necessarily to provide supporting fire, but rather to offer different positions from which a single mortar could operate at any one site, the weapon being moved around as the situation required. Many of these mountings were originally sunk in a pit, since filled in, to give some degree of protection to their crew. A pair on Salthouse Heath may still be seen in their original pits.[105]

*A spigot mortar base covering a road junction at Edgefield, near Holt* [106] *(1996)*

A Home Guard weapon, the spigot mortar is commonly thought to have had a limited range, and to have been inaccurate, slow, and dangerous to operate. But according to the American *Handbook on the British Army* (1942) the spigot mortar was 'A very good short range AT [anti-tank] weapon'.[107] And Churchill was highly impressed after seeing a demonstration, describing the spigot mortar as 'an excellent weapon'.[108] By July 1941 1,200 had been allotted to the Home Guard in Eastern Command, and a further 1,800 for the defence of aerodromes, nodal points, beach defences and so on.[109]

*Damage to this spigot mortar base near Great Yarmouth has revealed its solid construction* [110] *(1998)*

*One of two surviving slit trenches near North Walsham (1992)*

Slit trenches were built in large numbers. Being of a less permanent nature than pill-boxes they have not usually survived, or are very difficult to find. Two remain in fairly good condition at Little London,[111] near North Walsham, in front of a pillbox beside the B1150, showing how pillboxes were used in conjunction with other defences. Nearby is a Home Guard shelter, a small brick building with a concrete roof and two small windows at one end. This was a standardised design, sometimes known as an 'elephant hut'. Although very common they are easily overlooked, being much less distinctive than pillboxes.

Any large, smooth expanse of open ground could be used as a landing place for enemy gliders. The most common counter-measure was to dig a network of ditches 150 yards apart, in the layout of a right-angled grid. They were to be positioned mainly about five miles from the coast.[112] Digging the trenches required time and effort, however, and in reality all sorts of obstacles were used, including cars salvaged from the scrap heap!

Hickling Broad, the largest of the Norfolk Broads, offered a clear expanse of water on which enemy aircraft could land. Large motor cruisers from Herbert Woods' boatyard at nearby Potter Heigham were sunk across the broad to form an obstruction.[113] This actually did the boats surprisingly little damage; during the war no pleasure boating was allowed on the Broads, and had the wooden cruisers been out of the water altogether their planks would have shrunk, causing persistent leaks when they were next launched. Some of these scuttled boats, the *King of Light* class, are still cruising on the Broads today.

*Prince of Light, one of the boats sunk on Hickling Broad to prevent gliders landing, on the River Thurne (1998)*

## Unusual survivals

Several intriguing Second World War buildings that have not been mentioned above remain in Norfolk. A few rare survivals are described below, but many more lie buried in the vegetation for the keen researcher to discover.

A small concrete building may just be glimpsed beside Wood Lane in Kelling, near Weybourne.[114] Now very overgrown, this was a bunker for the crew and a generator for a dummy airfield at Salthouse, a decoy for the one at Langham. Runway lights powered from this building lured bombers away from Langham Airfield, and the Salthouse site was bombed in 1942.[115] Such night-time decoys were known as 'Q' sites.

At Langham Airfield [116] there remains a dome trainer (or astro dome), one of very few surviving nationally. It was a form of battle simulation used for training gunners, one of a number of systems used for synthetic training during the Second World War.[117] A gun turret was mounted in the floor, and images of attacking aircraft were projected onto the inside of the dome. Roly Millar, a glider pilot in the Second World War, remembers what it was like to use a small dome trainer at Brize Norton in Oxfordshire:

> The gun was close to the wall so that when the enemy aircraft came down the steep roof he was diving straight at you...Five or six of us went in at a time for instruction. We sat on the bench. The instructor gave us a demo. From his box he controlled the direction and speed of the aircraft. As well as that, by pressing a button, he made the noise of the aircraft firing at you if you missed. If it was going to pass sideways you swung the sights in line in front of him and fired...The first pupil took his stand behind the gun. Then a twelve inch aircraft flashed on the screen, emerged from the top of the wall and ascended the dome. The gunner's sights were also shown on the sky. Thus the instructor knew if the aim was good. The noise of the gun told him when you were firing.
>
> My turn next. The aircraft appeared on the opposite horizon. I was intrigued by it all. There was no sensation of a dome. Just a black aircraft coming at me fast from the far horizon. I lined

*A dome trainer still remaining at Langham Airfield (1996)*

up but was so fascinated by it all that I let him shoot first. He came straight at me. I was badly shot up but live to tell the tale.[118]

At the Langham dome the supports for the gun and the remains of the screen may still be seen. There were three dome trainers at Weybourne camp, for training the anti-aircraft gunners, but these no longer remain.[119]

Among the most secret Second World War organisations were British Resistance Units, the 'Secret Army'. These comprised specially trained and armed men who would go into hiding as soon as a German invasion got underway. They would then work as a better-equipped version of the French Resistance. The bases from which they were to operate had to be very well concealed. In total there were 36 bases in the Norfolk area.[120]

I was given details of two of the operational bases, one in Norwich and one in South Walsham, by Mr R.N.Evans of Thorpe. The Norwich base, in Belmore Plantation, off South Hill Road, had three rooms, connected by long passage-ways. There were two entrance hatches. The complex was just below ground level, covered with soil and pine needles. To give ventilation, some pine trees were cut down to their stumps, which were then hollowed out. The South Walsham base was near a bridge in 'Sots Hole' wood, beside the Ranworth Road.[121]

Mr Evans stumbled across the Norwich base in 1946, finding some hand grenades inside, about which he notified the police. It may seem surprising that these were left there after the whole organisation was wound up in 1944, but this case was nothing compared to the hoard removed from a milking shed in Dengie, Essex, in 1964. This included several thousand rounds of ammunition, hundreds of bombs and well over a tonne of high explosives![122] As recently as 1994 some two dozen phosphorus bombs, improvised from milk bottles, were found beside the A47 at Wendling, near Dereham.[123]

Mr Evans' uncle, who had been in the Home Guard during the war, accidentally came across the South Walsham bunker while it was under construction. He was sworn to secrecy, and was told that in the event of an invasion, he would have to come to the bunker himself, for security reasons, or he would be shot.[124] The Secret Army could not afford to risk detection at any price.

## The cost

An astonishing number of defences had been built mainly within the space of a few months. By 8th October 1940, 1,697 miles of wire, 73 miles of anti-tank mines and 440 miles of anti-tank obstacles had been put up in Eastern Command. And there was more still to be built. The work involved was staggering. In total, Eastern Command expected to have built 5,819 pillboxes, averaging 11 for every mile of beach - far more than for any other command.[125]

This vast construction programme cost a great deal of money, at a time when Great Britain could ill afford it. Eastern Command's approved expenditure on defence works to the end of 1941 totalled £3,745,000. The total for all the commands was £21,172,500.[126] Nor did the defence building finish there. Eastern Command estimated that they would have to spend a further £521,000 by the end of March 1942. But within months demolition work was to begin, also at great cost.

**Notes to The Second World War**

[1] PRO: WO 199/85, 4a.
[2] PRO: WO 199/85, 17.
[3] PRO: WO 199/85, 4a.
[4] TG 4991 1972.
[5] PRO: WO 199/85, 9a, 10a and 11a.
[6] PRO: WO 199/85, 17a.
[7] Peter Brooks, *Coastal Towns at War*, pp 10-11.
[8] PRO: WO 199/85, 17a.
[9] PRO: WO 199/2477, 19a.
[10] PRO: WO 199/95, 47a.
[11] TG 1113 4367.
[12] TG 5194 0790.
[13] IWM: H2701-2702.
[14] TG 2093 4206.
[15] PRO: WO 199/48, 1a.
[16] PRO: WO 287/84, ch 4, p 23.
[17] PRO: WO 192/67.
[18] TG 3750 3171.
[19] IWM: H12963 and H12953.
[20] PRO: WO 199/1176, 45a.
[21] PRO: WO 192/62.
[22] Letter from Henry Wills to author, 23rd March 1993.
[23] TG 4979 1921.
[24] P.W.Gee, *A History of the Essex Yeomanry 1919-1949: Part III*, pp 174-176.
[25] PRO: WO 32/11674, 36a.
[26] TG 3080 3719.
[27] PRO: WO 32/11674, 36a.
[28] NCC: Dep. 68. Letter from the County Planning Officer to the Regional Controller, 11th March 1948.
[29] Mentioned in PRO: WO 199/2528, 33b. It was on the south-west side of Wroxham Bridge: TG 3015 1805
[30] Reprinted in *Reflections on Intelligence* by R.V.Jones, p 334. Jones describes the report as 'probably the best single report received from any source during the war' (p 275), though originally the British largely ignored it.
[31] Measured drawings of types 22-26 are preserved in PRO: WO 199/1703, 6a.

[32] The thick-walled version found in Norfolk is sometimes erroneously identified as type 29 in modern literature; this is not an original designation and is avoided in this book.
[33] Mistakenly identified in *Pillboxes* by Henry Wills as a pair of type 26 pillboxes joined together.
[34] TG 3740 3171.
[35] PRO: WO 199/2567, 124.
[36] PRO: WO 199/1779, 8a.
[37] e.g. TM 4348 9081.
[38] TG 2950 3770.
[39] TG 0501 4526.
[40] PRO: WO 199/1779, 16a.
[41] PRO: WO 199/1779, 52a.
[42] TG 2646 1990.
[43] William Stibbons of Coltishall to author, May 1991.
[44] Henry Wills, *Pillboxes*, p 14.
[45] IWM: H5109.
[46] PRO: WO 199/44, 5b.
[47] e.g. TG 1161 4330.
[48] TG 1429 2759.
[49] *Loopholes: the Journal of the Pillbox Study Group*, ed. David Burridge, nos. 3-6, 8, 11.
[50] PRO: WO 199/44, 5b.
[51] PRO: WO 199/1779, 98a.
[52] PRO: WO 199/2, 41a.
[53] e.g. at West Raynham Airfield, TF 8558 2464
[54] TG 2683 2207.
[55] PRO: WO 199/1779, 97a.
[56] PRO: WO 199/1779, 104a.
[57] IWM: H12848.
[58] PRO: WO 199/1779, 82a.
[59] Illustrated in Peter Brooks, *Coastal Towns at War*, p 14.
[60] TG 0478 4441.
[61] PRO: WO 199/2527, 1b.
[62] PRO: WO 199/1779, 82a.
[63] PRO: WO 199/2527, 45a.
[64] TG 0010 1900 and TG 0011 1850.
[65] TG 2141 1356, TG 2204 1340 and TG 2244 1369.
[66] TG 2204 1340.
[67] PRO: WO 199/2527, 1a.
[68] Drawings of both designs are preserved in PRO: WO 199/2657. A drawing of the Norcon fully reinforced with sandbags is in WO 199/2527.

[69] PRO: WO 199/2527, 1a.
[70] TG 0931 4382.
[71] TG 2093 4206.
[72] I am grateful to Mr R.S.Symonds for sending me slides of these pillboxes taken shortly before their demolition.
[73] PRO: WO 199/1779.
[74] PRO: WO 199/2528, 1b.
[75] PRO: WO 199/1779, 61a.
[76] PRO: WO 199/1779, 123e.
[77] PRO: WO 199/44, 5b.
[78] TL 8750 8508.
[79] Letter from Alan Shaw to author, 17th May 1995.
[80] TG 1113 4367.
[81] Illustrated in Henry Wills, *Pillboxes*, p 62.
[82] IWM: H11909-11910.
[83] TG 4021 1063.
[84] TG 4180 0730.
[85] TG 4419 0899.
[86] TG 3718 1721.
[87] TG 3919 2518.
[88] TG 3475 3328.
[89] PRO: WO 199/1722.
[90] TF 6513 3340.
[91] TG 4991 1972.
[92] Letter from Alan Shaw to author, 17th May 1995.
[93] TG 2160 2537.
[94] TG 2258 2402.
[95] TG 3130 3690.
[96] TF 7645 1445.
[97] TF 6739 2562.
[98] IWM: H2711.
[99] Illustrated in PRO: WO 199/1722.
[100] TF 5055 0036.
[101] TG 1279 4361.
[102] PRO: WO 199/1722, 18a.
[103] IWM: H12852.
[104] PRO: WO 199/44, 5b.
[105] TG 0730 4301 and TG 0749 4290.
[106] TG 0910 3435.
[107] This is reprinted as *The British Army in WW II* by Brian L. Davis.

[108] R.S.Macrae, *Winston Churchill's Toyshop*, p 86.
[109] PRO: WO 199/2438, 18a.
[110] TG 5152 1463.
[111] TG 2962 3130.
[112] Letter from Kate Sussams to author, 15th June 1995.
[113] Kim Dowe of Potter Heigham to author, August 1996.
[114] TG 0894 4284.
[115] *Decoy Sites* by Huby Fairhead, p 18. There is a photograph and a plan of the building on p 19.
[116] TF 9917 4191.
[117] Others are illustrated and described in *British Airfield Buildings of the Second World War* by Graham Buchan Innes, pp 64-76.
[118] Letter to author, 1st July 1998.
[119] Marked on a map in the archives of the Walpole family at Wolterton Hall: 10/52.
[120] Adrian Hoare, *Standing up to Hitler*, p 222. This book gives further details of the Secret Army and contains many personal accounts by those who were members of it.
[121] Information from Mr R.N.Evans of Thorpe to author, 2nd July 1995.
[122] Derek Johnson, *East Anglia at War*, pp 31-32.
[123] Reported in the *Eastern Daily Press*, 20th August 1994.
[124] Mr Evans to author, 2nd July 1995.
[125] PRO: WO 199/48, 43a.
[126] PRO: WO 199/48, 6a.

# DEMOLITION AND DECAY

In the space of a few months Norfolk's picturesque landscape had been transformed into a deadly network of gun batteries, pillboxes, anti-tank obstacles, trenches, barbed wire and mines. An enormous amount of time, money and effort had been channelled into the construction programme. More than anything, the sheer scale of it epitomised the will to resist the invader. But the demolition of the defences got under way even before the war was over.

From 1943 the coastal batteries were handed over to the Home Guard, and later kept in a state of care and maintenance. The reduction of the batteries (known as the 'Neaptide' reductions) left only the Gorleston Pier battery operational, with the Links battery at Great Yarmouth being retained for practice.[1] As for the others, Hunstanton and Sheringham had already been closed. Towards the end of 1944 arrangements were made to remove almost all equipment except the main armament from the remaining batteries,[2] and the guns were scrapped after the end of the war.[3]

*The remains of one of the gun platforms at Cley battery,[4] the mounting for a 6-inch gun clearly visible (1993)*

In May 1943 the Major-General commanding the Norfolk and Cambridge District wrote 'It is agreed that in non-coastal areas pillboxes which encroach on highways, and which serve no useful purposes operationally in the present defence schemes, should be demolished'.[5]

The removal of inland defences was also under way before the war ended, though the Brigadier of the General Staff, Eastern Command, specified that no military labour was to be used for such demolition work. At this stage it was principally a few troublesome pillboxes that were in question, rather than an organised programme of 'cleaning up the countryside'.

In particular a pillbox at Fakenham, built in the market place and disguised with a statue of Justicia on its roof, was proving troublesome.[6] The Clerk of Walsingham District Council wrote to the War Office to complain that it persistently caused 'traffic blocks of considerable dimensions', and was a constant danger to pedestrians, as lorries had to mount the pavement to get round it.[7] Since it was now December 1943, it was finally decided that the pillbox did not have a significant role to play in the defence of the country, and could be removed. But by July 1944 the pillbox was still in place; a shortage of labour meant it was not possible for the Divisional Road Engineer to carry out the work he had undertaken. The file records nothing further, but the pillbox no longer remains today.

By this stage in the war the priorities were clear. All commands were sent a letter informing them that 'In view of the fact that there is a serious shortage of wire netting throughout the country which is urgently needed for chicken runs, rabbit netting etc. it has been decided that the wire netting used on pillboxes for camouflage purposes is no longer necessary as although in most cases the wire netting is still good the camouflage material which was mounted on it has deteriorated so badly that it has almost disappeared.'[8]

As early as 1943 work began on the daunting project of lifting the mines that had been laid on beaches all around the country. After years of coastal erosion and shifting sands the original perimeters of the minefields could not be relied upon. Major Alan Shaw of the Royal Engineers, involved in clearing the mines, remembers 'In 1940 the pressure to lay mines quickly resulted in many minefields being laid both on beaches and inland by personnel without the equipment or skill to make accurate minefield location drawings. Sometimes the trace wires intended to enable them to be relocated safely were broken or non-existent.[9] To make matters worse, the gelignite primers had by now become unstable, and the mines were even more lethal than they had been in 1940.

The task facing Bomb Disposal was monumental, but 290,000 mines had been cleared nationwide by early 1946, leaving only 35,000. However by August a total of 140 men had been killed in this work, and 46 injured. One of those who lost their lives was a German prisoner of war, for volunteer PoWs were helping to clear the mines, and had made twenty minefields safe by early 1948.[10] In October 1946, Bomb Disposal was able to recommend that only three minefields be closed indefinitely, at Folkestone, Hastings, and at Trimingham in Norfolk. It appears that the dangerous areas were not sufficiently barricaded off, however, for the following year a holidaymaker was blown up by a mine lodged in the cliff at Trimingham. It was believed that around 1,000 live mines were still lying just beneath the sand between Trimingham and Sidestrand, and this minefield came to be regarded as the most dangerous in the whole of Britain.

Trimingham, Overstrand and Salthouse became notorious for the difficulty of keeping them clear of mines. Constant re-sweeping was necessary, for at Salthouse the tide would reach under the large shingle bank and keep bringing up more mines. 150 men were employed on the clearance of this minefield alone.[11] At Weybourne, four thousand mines were cleared from a four-mile stretch of beach, at the cost of fourteen armoured bulldozers.[12] Erosion could bring to light minefields which had been laid inland, and despite the heroic efforts of Bomb Disposal it was impossible to guarantee that all the mines had been cleared. As recently as 1997 a live mine was found on the beach at Sheringham.[13] Trimingham and Sidestrand beaches were not reopened to the public until 1966, after a total of 530 mines had been removed.[14]

With the VE Day celebrations scarcely over, a conference was held in July 1945 at the Norwich offices of Captain Winterton, the War Department Land Agent for Norfolk, to determine what was to be done about the defences.[15] It was estimated that around 1,000 miles of derelict barbed wire were left in Norfolk, most of which Captain Winterton announced would be left for the time being.

*The shell of a pillbox, now upside down, at Weybourne Hope.*[16] *The beach here is littered with often unintelligible concrete remains. Part of a type 28 pillbox can be seen on the left. (1997)*

However, an attempt to remove all wire on arable or pasture land as quickly as possible was already in progress. The intention was to provide farmers with the necessary facilities for doing this, and to cover the costs they incurred. The War Department would pay Local Authorities for the cost of removing wire from seaside resorts. The wire was to be buried in anti-tank ditches or dumped in wasteland.The report states that all the anti-tank ditches in Norfolk had been filled in, while 95% of aircraft landing obstructions had already been removed. However an anti-tank ditch still survives near Weybourne (see illustration on page 42).

The Ministry of War Transport was taking care of the demolition of pillboxes on public highways, as well as the filling in of slit trenches. Private contractors were able to remove a pillbox for approximately £40, a marked saving on the cost of £120 for each pillbox clearance incurred by the Highway Authorities. Spigot mortar sites were being filled in for £7 or £8 each. Brick ammunition buildings were to be sold to the public, but steel ones returned to store.

*A pair of spigot mortar bases which came to light recently at Walcott.*[17] *It is possible they were buried after the war as an easy way of disposing of them. (1998)*

There was a lot of confusion in Norfolk County Council about which sites should be demolished urgently, which should be demolished at some future date, but not immediately, and which could be left. The Ministry of Town and Country Planning issued an official categorisation in December 1947 to clarify the situation.[18] Any defence which was dangerous to man or beast, interfered with recreation, impeded approved development, contravened bye-laws or was a public nuisance (such as the Fakenham pillbox, it appears!) was to be removed. If the demolition of a defence was not in the national interest, or if the cost of demolition was out of all proportion to the benefits of removal, the defence was to stay. However in February 1951 the County Planning Officer noted that the categorisation was still being changed.[19]

*This lump of concrete on the beach near Weybourne is still just identifiable as the remnant of a pillbox by its distinctive loophole.*[20] *(1999)*

In cases where the War Department decided that a defence did not warrant demolition, the Department was supposed to pay compensation to the owner of the land, which was in the region of £5. As the figures above show, this was grossly inadequate for the demolition of a pillbox, and may instead have been regarded as simply a compensation for nuisance. John Wright, making enquiries in North Norfolk in 1964, found no owner who remembered having been paid compensation, and concluded that if it ever was paid out it may have been included in the repurchase price of the land.[21]

Some of the coastal defences were allowed to remain for the purposes of sea defence. The casemates of Cley battery had been built into the earth bank, and the County Planning Officer was told that this would be weakened by their removal. On the other hand, other parts of the battery were recommended for demolition because they interfered with sea defence, such as the gun platforms themselves.[22] In practice, however, the gun platforms remained untouched until recently (illustrated on page 54). Docking Rural District Council suggested that some of the anti-boat scaffolding at Brancaster should remain (as it did until a few years ago), since its removal would damage the sand dunes. The seaward loopholes of two pillboxes built into the sea wall were to be sealed up, however, to prevent the sea penetrating behind the wall.[23]

*A pillbox incorporated into modern sea defences at Eccles [24] (1998)*

By 1964, the County Planning Officer announced that 700 items remained in Norfolk awaiting clearance, out of the 14,000 that had originally been classified. Many of these were 'small and quite inoffensive objects' such as spigot mortar bases.[25]

One of the few people to look upon the defences with an eye for posterity was Lord Fisher, who at his request was given permission in December 1946 to preserve a pillbox on his land at Croxton, near Thetford, as a war memento.[26] This survives to this day.[27]

Today the surviving defences are often buried deep in the undergrowth. Any original use of natural camouflage becomes more effective over the years. Pillboxes can become completely invisible even to the best trained eye and the most rigorous investigator. A pillbox at Wroxham, for example, has sunk completely into the ground.[28] It is possible to be standing on top of a pillbox without knowing it - I have done so on more than one occasion, even when I have been looking for that very pillbox.

*A now all-but-invisible heavy machine-gun pillbox at Salthouse, with only the entrance showing [29] (1993)*

Vegetation is not the only hindrance to tracking down the defences. Pillboxes turn up in a wide variety of places. In consequence, being attacked by a horse, becoming entangled in an electric fence and in rusty barbed wire, nearly falling over hundred-foot cliffs, and being assaulted by flying golf balls have all had to be endured for the sake of this book.

Many coastal defences have tumbled over the cliffs or have been demolished before they can do so. Even during the war coastal erosion was a problem, causing a searchlight at Mundesley to be endangered,[30] and leading to the closure of the battery at Hunstanton.[31] The underground magazines of the batteries have usually been filled in, and the casemates demolished or converted for modern use. The best remaining batteries are at King's Lynn,[32] Brancaster,[33] Mundesley[34] and Happisburgh,[35] though most of Cley battery survived until a few years ago.[36] Mundesley battery remains almost intact, despite being given priority for demolition in early 1945, owing to the erosion.[37] It was still possible to enter the magazines and shelters at Brancaster on my last visit there in 1994, and to walk all the way between the casemates underground.

The beaches themselves yield the occasional wartime relic. In lonelier areas rusty pieces of beach scaffolding may still be found, and in some places pillboxes and anti-tank blocks lie at alarming angles on the shifting sands. During a storm at Caister in April 1996, fifteen feet of sand was removed by the sea, revealing a pillbox which had sunk from view in the 1950s.[38] When I went to record this site four months later the pillbox had almost completely disappeared into the sand again. In the space of a few years, the remains on Weybourne beach have become unrecognisable as pillboxes. Lashed again and again by the sea, the concrete has gradually disintegrated and is swallowed up by the sand. The carefully camouflaged heavy machine-gun emplacement built into the

*A heavy machine-gun pillbox at Caister. Completely buried for forty years, it came to light after a storm in 1996, but when this photograph was taken, was rapidly disappearing once more (1996)*

cliff above is edging ever closer to destruction. Below it are the remains of other pillboxes that have already crashed down on to the beach.

*A Home Guard shelter at Letheringsett put to a peacetime use*[39] *(1993)*

Some of the old defences can be found still fulfilling a useful function today. Home Guard shelters make excellent garden sheds, or even, in some cases, cattle shelters.

Pillboxes themselves, however, with their unusual shapes and internal walls are less useful for peacetime purposes, but some have

*A spigot mortar base on the River Ant at Wayford Bridge in use as a mooring post. It has since disappeared.*[41] *(1992)*

had their baffle walls removed and are used as tool stores. A garden shed at Meeting House Hill, near North Walsham, is just recognisable as having once been a standard pillbox.[40] The original function of the defences is easily forgotten. The spikes of spigot mortar bases by the river are convenient for tying up boats, though boat hirers are often puzzled as to why some boatyards have taken the trouble to provide such an excessively heavy-duty mooring post for them.

It is fashionable today to sneer at the fortifications built to save the British from a Nazi invasion. The popular image of Britain's state of readiness in 1940 is of Captain Mainwaring's steadfast but bumbling platoon. But few people realise the extent of the measures planned against invasion. The beaches were to be swamped with mustard gas, contravening the Geneva Protocol; a scorched earth policy was considered.[42] The scale of the preparation even went as far as making arrangements to destroy carrier pigeons and their lofts in areas where invasion was considered imminent.[43]

Pillboxes are the only commonly seen remnant of the defence network. When we see a derelict pillbox standing isolated in the middle of a field today, it is important to remember that we cannot see the trenches, barbed wire, anti-tank blocks, spigot mortar bases and even flame throwers that might originally have accompanied it, and to recall that the bridge it covered would have been mined, while the river below would have been impassable for enemy tanks.

Despite their often battered appearance, with the concrete having cracked between each poured layer, many pillboxes have withstood the test of time remarkably well. At Happisburgh, for example, a pillbox may be seen on the beach having tumbled from the high cliffs without any discernible damage, even though it has landed upside down. Demolishing the defences is no easy task almost sixty years after they were built, as road-builders today often find. A thick-walled pillbox at Thursford,[44] near Fakenham, took a week to remove.[45]

Pillboxes are still built today. The small 'Sangers' found protecting military airfields and radar stations are based on the Norcon pillbox, made from a concrete pipe. Otherwise the different nature of modern warfare makes it unlikely that the kinds of defence built in such vast quantities sixty years ago will ever be constructed again. Even before the war was over they were regarded as deathtraps for their crews. But they form a part of Britain's defence history that has been largely ignored by posterity, despite the great number surviving. The old defences serve as a reminder of the resolve of the people who lived through one of the most desperate periods in British history.

*The foundations of a small pillbox at Weybourne being swallowed up by the sea [46] (1998)*

## Notes to Decay and Demolition

[1] PRO: WO 199/2452, 61b.
[2] PRO: WO 199/2452.
[3] Peter Kent, *Fortifications of East Anglia,* p 194.
[4] TG 0501 4530.
[5] PRO: WO 199/2528, 27a.
[6] Illustrated in J.Baldwin and A.Tickle, *Memories of Fakenham Lancaster,* p 8.
[7] PRO: WO 199/2528, 58a.
[8] PRO: WO 199/2528, 82.
[9] Letter to author, 17th May 1995.
[10] *Sunday Express,* 29th February 1948.
[11] John Frayn Turner, *Highly Explosive,* ch 6.
[12] *Sunday Express*, 29th February 1948.

[13] *Eastern Daily Press*, 5th August 1997.
[14] *Eastern Daily Press*, 29th July 1966.
[15] NCC: Dep. 68 16 TG 1120 4374.
[16] TG 1117 4370
[17] TG 3590 3291.
[18] NCC: Dep. 68.
[19] NCC: Dep. 68, 6287.
[20] TG 1271 4369.
[21] Note in John Wright's papers, 21st February 1964.
[22] NCC: Dep. 68. Letter from the Chief Engineer of the North Norfolk Catchment Board to the County Planning Officer, 30th November1950.
[23] NCC: Dep. 68, 6073.
[24] TG 4030 2962.
[25] NCC: Dep. 68. Letter to Mrs Ida J.Tinkler, 6th April 1964.
[26] Mentioned in a list of sites compiled by John Wright from parish files in NCC.
[27] TL 8750 8508.
[28] TG 2965 1689.
[29] TG 0728 4394.
[30] PRO: WO 199/1176.
[31] Peter Kent, *Fortifications of East Anglia*, p 194.
[32] TF 5859 2441.
[33] TF 7732 4517.
[34] TG 3080 3719.
[35] TG 3750 3171.
[36] 'Norfolk and Suffolk Coast Defence Study' by Jeff Dorman, *Ravelin*, no. 19, October 1989. When this survey was made most of the battery was still extant. The battery observation post was blown up in 1955 (reported in the *Eastern Daily Press*, 15th August 1955).
[37] PRO: WO 199/2452, 87.
[38] TG 5259 1269.
[39] TG 0600 3875.
[40] TG 3060 2825.
[41] TG 3489 2478.
[42] PRO: WO 199/179.
[43] PRO: WO 199/179, 30a.
[44] TF 9939 3370.
[45] Information from Mr D.Bailey of Thursford to author, May 1995.
[46] TG 1271 4371.

# GAZETTEER

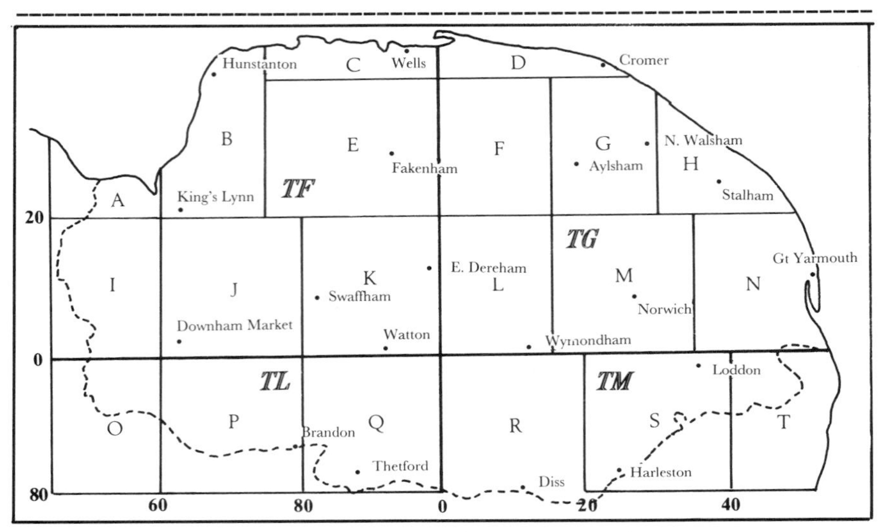


This gazetteer of 1042 sites covers all the fixed defences known to have been built in Norfolk in the First and Second World Wars and is far more extensive than those hitherto published. Since the gazetteer also covers many sites demolished decades ago it is hoped it is largely complete, although a few sites have had to be omitted where there was insufficient evidence to determine their location satisfactorily. Many sites were destroyed during the ten-year period of work on the gazetteer; those known to have been demolished at the time of publication are marked in italics. The sectors A-T refer to the 20 sectors into which the county is divided in the map

Very few grid references showing where Norfolk's defences were built appear to have survived among the War Office papers at the Public Record Office (if, indeed, they were ever officially recorded in the first place). For the most part these sites had to be located by fieldwork. The work was carried out by Peter Kent, Simon Purcell, Mike Osborne, Philippa Miller and Christopher Bird. Papers preserved by John Wright were very helpful in adding long-vanished sites to the list. Peter Kent undertook the major task of co-ordinating the project and organising the data.

No doubt before long many more of these defences will have succumbed to demolition. It is hoped that this gazetteer will provide a permanent record of Norfolk's defence system.

---

# *KEY*

---

| | |
|---|---|
| ATB | Anti-tank block |
| ATD | Anti-tank ditch |
| ATR | Anti-tank rail |
| AW | Alan Williams turret |
| BB | Blacker bombard spigot mortar emplacement |
| BHQ | Battle headquarters |
| CB | Coastal battery |
| CDL or SL | Coast defence searchlight |
| CSP | Converted strongpoint |
| CWM | Concrete weapon mounting |
| DP | Defence post |
| EH | Engine house (for CDL) |
| GE | Gun emplacement |
| GP | Gun position |
| HAA | Heavy anti-aircraft battery |
| HGS | Home Guard shelter |
| HMG | Heavy machine-gun emplacement |
| L | L-shaped section pillbox |
| LAA | Light anti-aircraft battery |
| LH | Loophole |
| NOR | Norcon pillbox |
| OP | Observation post |
| PH | Pickett-Hamilton pillbox |
| PB? | Unknown type of pillbox |
| PBX | Non-standard design of pillbox |
| RN | Royal Navy pattern of pillbox |
| S | Shelter |
| SHB | Super heavy battery (inland) |
| SM | Spigot mortar base |
| ST | Slit trench |
| SP | Strongpoint |
| W1A | Circular World War I pillbox |
| W1B | Hexagonal World War I pillbox |
| WM | Weapon mount |
| 20 | Heavy machine-gun pillbox, here called Type 20 |

# *KEY (cont.)*

| | |
|---|---|
| 2/20 | Pillbox made from two type 20s |
| 22 | Type 22 pillbox |
| 23 | Type 23 pillbox |
| 24 | Type 24 pillbox |
| 25 | Type 25 pillbox |
| 26 | Type 26 pillbox |
| 27 | Type 27 pillbox |
| 28 | Type 28 pillbox |

N.B. Sites from one parish may occur in more than one sector.

## Sector A

| Parish | Type | Map Ref. |
|---|---|---|
| Clenchwarton | CB | TF 5859 2441 |
| Clenchwarton | PBX | TF 5879 2419 |
| Terrington St Clem. | 23 | TF 5265 2530 |
| Terrington St Clem. | 22 | TF 5339 2430 |
| Terrington St Clem. | 22 | TF 5341 2441 |

## Sector B

| Parish | Type | Map Ref. |
|---|---|---|
| Castle Rising | ATB | TF 6739 2562 |
| Dersingham | 22 | TF 6809 3075 |
| *Grimston* | *PB?* | *TF 7029 2203* |
| *Heacham* | *PB?* | *TF 6520 3468* |
| Heacham | ATB | TF 6625 3686 |
| Heacham | 28 | TF 6632 3686 |
| Heacham | SM | TF 6632 3685 |
| Heacham | 28 | TF 6635 3680 |
| Hillingdon | HGS | TF 7277 2619 |
| Holme | 22 | TF 6854 4298 |
| *Holme* | *22* | *TF 6958 4416* |
| Holme | SM | TF 6946 4403 |
| Holme | SM | TF 6968 4425 |
| Holme | HGS | TF 6973 4395 |
| Holme | 28 | TF 6995 4350 |
| Holme | S | TF 7065 4455 |
| Holme | S | TF 7109 4493 |
| Holme | S | TF 7114 4496 |
| Holme | SM | TF 7222 4438 |
| *Holme* | *AW* | *TF 6935 4388* |
| *Holme* | *AW* | *TF 6930 4385* |
| Holme | SM | TF 6946 4403 |
| Holme | SM | TF 6968 4425 |
| *Hunstanton* | *CB* | *TF 6753 4196* |
| Hunstanton | RN | TF 6766 4210 |
| *Hunstanton* | *PB?* | *TF 6800 4243* |
| Hunstanton | 22 | TF 6874 4253 |
| *Hunstanton* | *AW* | *TF 3869 4283* |
| *Hunstanton* | *SM* | *TF 3871 4284* |
| King's Lynn | SM | TF 6256 2045 |
| Shernborne | 22 | TF 7145 3127 |
| Snettisham | ATB | TF 6513 3340 |
| Snettisham | HGS | TF 6558 3351 |
| *Thornham* | *AW* | *TF 7340 4490* |
| West Lynn | ATR | TF 6025 1995 |
| West Newton | 22 | TF 6945 2616 |
| Wormegay | ATB | TF 6698 1351 |

## Sector C

| Parish | Type | Map Ref. |
|---|---|---|
| Brancaster | 28 | TF 7702 4431 |
| Brancaster | 24 | TF 7740 4421 |
| Brancaster | 20 | TF 7705 4512 |
| Brancaster | SM | TF 7705 4513 |
| Brancaster | 24 | TF 7705 4514 |
| Brancaster | 20 | TF 7700 4518 |
| Brancaster | CB | TF 7732 4517 |
| *Brancaster* | *CDL* | *TF 7778 4533* |
| *Brancaster* | *AW* | *TF 7700 4513* |
| *Brancaster* | *SM* | *TF 7702 4513* |
| *Brancaster* | *PB?* | *TF 7712 4475* |
| *Brancaster* | *AW* | *TF 7762 4526* |
| *Brancaster* | *PB?* | *TF 7769 4527* |
| *Brancaster* | *PB?* | *TF 7772 4528* |
| Burnham Market | 22 | TF 8149 4165 |
| Burnham Market | PBX | TF 8258 4201 |
| Burnham Market | 22 | TF 8261 4183 |
| *Burnham Market* | *PB?* | *TF 8359 4188* |
| Burnham Norton | ATB | TF 8350 4344 |
| Burnham Norton | SM | TF 8350 4282 |
| Burnham Norton | SM | TF 8352 4264 |
| Burnham Overy | SM | TF 8502 4491 |
| Choseley | 22 | TF 7555 4073 |
| Holkham | ATB | TF 8780 4407 |
| Holkham | 2/20 | TF 8795 4495 |
| Holkham | 2/20 | TF 8795 4426 |
| Holkham | 2/20 | TF 8907 4435 |
| Holkham | 2/20 | TF 8928 4426 |
| Holkham | AW | TF 8970 4387 |
| *Holkham* | *CB* | *TF 9050 4585* |
| *Holkham* | *PB?* | *TF 8832 4528* |
| *Holkham* | *PB?* | *TF 8845 4525* |
| *Holkham* | *PB?* | *TF 9014 4287* |
| *Holkham* | *PB?* | *TF 9022 4591* |
| Stiffkey | 22 | TF 9748 4227 |
| Stiffkey | W1A | TF 9675 4399 |
| Stiffkey | BHQ | TF 9990 4181 |
| Titchwell | S | TF 7503 4436 |
| Titchwell | S | TF 7512 4472 |
| Titchwell | GP | TF 7512 4486 |
| Warham | SM | TF 9495 4174 |
| Wells | 2/20 | TF 9129 4421 |
| Wells | 2/20 | TF 9131 4415 |
| *Wells* | *SM* | *TF 9155 4555* |

## Sector D

| Parish | Type | Map Ref. |
|---|---|---|
| Aylmerton | W1A | TG 1832 4051 |
| Cley | AW | TG 0478 4441 |
| Cley | 24 | TG 0512 4409 |
| Cley | 27 | TG 0501 4526 |
| Cley | CB | TG 0501 4530 |
| *Cley* | *PB?* | *TG 0439 4520* |
| *Cley* | *PB?* | *TG 0512 4520* |
| Cley | WM | TG 0530 4530 |
| *Cley* | *SM* | *TG 0475 4525* |
| *Cley* | *SM* | *TG 0442 4381* |
| *Cley* | *SM* | *TG 0457 4406* |
| Cley | HGS | TG 0481 4405 |
| Cromer | 20 | TG 2083 4203 |
| Cromer | SM | TG 2084 4203 |
| Cromer | L | TG 2093 4206 |
| Cromer | 22 | TG 2104 4206 |
| *Cromer* | *AW* | *TG 2107 4245* |
| *Cromer* | *AW* | *TG 2135 4248* |
| *Cromer* | *22* | *TG 2135 4248* |
| Cromer | 22 | TG 2154 4202 |
| Cromer | 22 | TG 2161 4167 |
| Cromer | HGS | TG 2158 4196 |
| Cromer | LH | TG 2178 4211 |
| Cromer | LH | TG 2212 4221 |
| *Cromer* | *CB* | *TG 2253 4199* |
| Cromer | 22 | TG 2270 4170 |
| *Cromer* | *22* | *TG 2219 4218* |
| Glandford | AW | TG 0484 4083 |
| Glandford | AW | TG 0499 4014 |
| *Glandford* | *AW* | *TG 0520 4040* |
| Kelling | 24 | TG 0885 4292 |
| Kelling | 2/20 | TG 0900 4299 |
| Kelling | 24 | TG 0908 4298 |
| Kelling | NOR | TG 0931 4382 |
| Kelling | 20 | TG 0957 4378 |
| Kelling | 22 | TG 0968 4406 |
| *Kelling* | *PB?* | *TG 0952 4397* |
| Kelling | 20 | TG 0962 4383 |
| Kelling | HAA | TG 0969 4382 |
| Kelling | HMG | TG 0984 4382 |
| Kelling | 20 | TG 0985 4385 |
| Kelling | 24 | TG 0998 4232 |
| Kelling | ST | TG 1042 4194 |
| Kelling | 2/20 | TG 1039 4284 |
| Langham | 22 | TG 0133 4177 |
| Overstrand | 22 | TG 2360 4089 |
| Runton | W1A | TG 1795 4298 |
| Runton | ST | TG 1834 4208 |
| Runton | 22 | TG 1876 4321 |
| Runton | ST | TG 2005 4197 |
| Runton | 22 | TG 2050 4275 |
| *Runton* | *PB?* | *TG 1855 4321* |
| *Runton* | *PB?* | *TG 1961 4295* |
| Salthouse | 26 | TG 0701 4388 |
| Salthouse | 24 | TG 0711 4376 |
| Salthouse | 20 | TG 0728 4394 |
| Salthouse | 20 | TG 0728 4392 |
| Salthouse | 22 | TG 0728 4396 |
| Salthouse | ATB | TG 0737 4399 |
| *Salthouse* | *ATR* | *TG 0730 4463* |
| Salthouse | AW | TG 0715 4305 |
| *Salthouse* | *20* | *TG 0736 4320* |
| Salthouse | SM | TG 0730 4301 |
| Salthouse | SM | TG 0749 4290 |
| *Salthouse* | *W1A* | *TG 0715 4460* |
| Salthouse | ATB | TG 0764 4392 |
| Salthouse | 20 | TG 0779 4432 |
| Salthouse | SM | TG 0777 4433 |
| *Salthouse* | *PB?* | *TG 0811 4440* |
| Salthouse | ATB | TG 0779 4387 |
| Salthouse | SM | TG 0857 4421 |
| Salthouse | 20 | TG 0861 4414 |
| Salthouse | 26 | TG 0917 4372 |
| Salthouse | ST | TG 0756 4316 |
| Salthouse | ST | TG 0760 4310 |
| Salthouse | ST | TG 0766 4306 |
| Salthouse | GP | TG 0768 4219 |
| Salthouse | GP | TG 0763 4229 |
| Salthouse | GP | TG 0762 4233 |
| Salthouse | GP | TG 0767 4240 |
| Salthouse | GP | TG 0761 4242 |
| Salthouse | GP | TG 0768 4215 |
| Salthouse | GO | TG 0772 4211 |
| *Salthouse* | *PB?* | *TG 0806 4431* |
| *Salthouse* | *SM* | *TG 0806 4429* |
| *Salthouse* | *PB?* | *TG 0812 4429* |
| *Salthouse* | *PB?* | *TG 0814 4431* |
| *Salthouse* | *SM* | *TG 0862 4415* |
| *Salthouse* | *DP* | *TG 0868 4420* |
| *Salthouse* | *PB?* | *TG 0872 4419* |
| *Salthouse* | *PB?* | *TG 0870 4421* |
| *Salthouse* | *PB?* | *TG 0869 4422* |
| *Salthouse* | *PB?* | *TG 0860 4420* |
| Sheringham | 22 | TG 1437 4353 |
| Sheringham | CB | TG 1489 4342 |
| *Sheringham* | *PB?* | *TG 1442 4352* |
| *Sheringham* | *PB?* | *TG 1496 4352* |

| Parish | Type | Map Ref. |
|---|---|---|
| Sheringham | ATB | TG 1564 4304 |
| *Sheringham* | *SM* | *TG 1567 4350* |
| *Sheringham* | *PB?* | *TG 1585 4234* |
| *Sheringham* | *PB?* | *TG 1645 4220* |
| Sheringham | W1A | TG 1675 4171 |
| Sheringham | GP | TG 1678 4330 |
| *Sheringham* | *PB?* | *TG 1695 4324* |
| Upper Sheringham | 22 | TG 1280 4364 |
| Upper Sheringham | SM | TG 1285 4364 |
| Upper Sheringham | 20 | TG 1322 4259 |
| Upper Sheringham | 20 | TG 1324 4276 |
| Upper Sheringham | 20 | TG 1327 4318 |
| Upper Sheringham | 20 | TG 1327 4323 |
| *Upper Sheringham* | *PB?* | *TG 1400 4100* |
| *Upper Sheringham* | *24* | *TG 1403 4291* |
| Upper Sheringham | SM | TG 1317 4255 |
| *Upper Sheringham* | *AW* | *TG 1329 4288* |
| Upper Sheringham | HGS | TG 1424 4188 |
| Weybourne | OP | TG 0988 4338 |
| Weybourne | GE | TG 0988 4339 |
| Weybourne | GP | TG 0987 4389 |
| Weybourne | 22 | TG 1011 4391 |
| Weybourne | 20 | TG 1028 4381 |
| Weybourne | HMG | TG 1025 4377 |
| Weybourne | 20 | TG 1022 4370 |
| Weybourne | W1A | TG 1021 4334 |
| *Weybourne* | *20* | *TG 1102 4376* |
| Weybourne | 20 | TG 1105 4376 |
| Weybourne | 20 | TG 1113 4367 |
| Weybourne | CDL | TG 1115 4372 |
| *Weybourne* | *PB?* | *TG 1117 4370* |
| Weybourne | 28 | TG 1117 4373 |
| Weybourne | SM | TG 1130 4143 |
| Weybourne | 24 | TG 1132 4352 |
| Weybourne | 26 | TG 1134 4326 |
| Weybourne | SM | TG 1135 4372 |
| Weybourne | ST | TG 1145 4360 |
| Weybourne | 2/20 | TG 1160 4349 |
| Weybourne | SM | TG 1160 4321 |
| Weybourne | 26 | TG 1161 4293 |
| Weybourne | 26 | TG 1161 4330 |
| Weybourne | 2/20 | TG 1164 4182 |
| Weybourne | 22 | TG 1179 4197 |
| Weybourne | 20 | TG 1195 4131 |
| Weybourne | 22 | TG 1235 4363 |
| Weybourne | 24 | TG 1240 4331 |
| Weybourne | 26 | TG 1240 4326 |
| Weybourne | SM | TG 1250 4365 |
| Weybourne | 24 | TG 1265 4354 |
| Weybourne | 26 | TG 1268 4350 |
| Weybourne | ATD | TG 1279 4361 |
| *Weybourne* | *PB?* | *TG 1271 4371* |
| *Weybourne* | *ATB* | *TG 1031 4326* |
| Weybourne | SM | TG 1033 4308 |
| *Weybourne* | *PB?* | *TG 1145 4370* |
| Weybourne | SM | TG 1199 4134 |
| Wiveton | 24 | TG 0434 4265 |

## Sector E

| Parish | Type | Map Ref. |
|---|---|---|
| Barsham | 22 | TF 9003 3580 |
| Binham | HGS | TF 9815 3983 |
| Bircham Newton | 22 | TF 7755 3406 |
| Bircham Newton | 22 | TF 7845 3366 |
| *Bircham Newton* | *PB?* | *TF 7955 3470* |
| Brisley | 22 | TF 9566 2146 |
| Docking | NOR | TF 7683 3683 |
| Docking | NOR | TF 7862 3685 |
| Docking | HGS | TF 7651 3673 |
| Docking | HGS | TF 7650 3673 |
| Docking | SM | TF 7671 3723 |
| Docking | 22 | TF 7814 3942 |
| Docking | 22 | TF 7874 3964 |
| Fulmodeston | SM | TF 9924 3120 |
| Great Walsingham | 24 | TF 9072 3749 |
| Great Walsingham | 24 | TF 9090 3750 |
| Great Walsingham | 24 | TF 9064 3740 |
| Great Walsingham | SM | TF 9090 3750 |
| Great Walsingham | SM | TF 9089 3749 |
| Great Walsingham | HGS | TF 9079 3746 |
| Guist | 22 | TF 9935 2590 |
| Guist | SM | TF 9995 2561 |
| *Guist* | *PB?* | *TF 9920 2740* |
| Hindringham | 24 | TF 9750 3613 |
| *Hindringham* | *PB?* | *TF 9850 3686* |
| Hindringham | HGS | TF 9861 3690 |
| *Hindringham* | *PB?* | *TF 9330 3590* |
| *Kettlestone* | *PB?* | *TF 9672 3164* |
| *Little Snoring* | *BHQ* | *TF 9580 3310* |
| *Little Snoring* | *CWM* | *TF 9560 3145* |
| *Little Snoring* | *CWM* | *TF 9561 3145* |
| Little Walsingham | 22 | TF 9405 3650 |
| Massingham | LAA | TF 8127 2424 |
| Massingham | 22 | TF 7781 2188 |
| Pudding Norton | 22 | TF 9348 2690 |
| Raynham | 22 | TF 8359 2512 |
| Raynham | 22 | TF 8378 2458 |
| Raynham | 22 | TF 8403 2417 |
| Raynham | 22 | TF 8453 2392 |
| Raynham | 22 | TF 8405 2552 |

| Parish | Type | Map Ref. |
|---|---|---|
| Raynham | 22 | TF 8478 2512 |
| Raynham | 22 | TF 8556 2361 |
| Raynham | 22 | TF 8539 2518 |
| Raynham | 25 | TF 8525 2396 |
| Raynham | BHQ | TF 8558 2464 |
| Raynham | 25 | TF 8583 2463 |
| Raynham | HGS | TF 8750 2520 |
| Raynham | 22 | TF 8835 2473 |
| Raynham | 22 | TF 8860 2460 |
| Raynham | 22 | TF 8858 2478 |
| Stanfield | 22 | TF 9285 2135 |
| *Stibbard* | *SL* | *TF 9907 2722* |
| *Stibbard* | *PB?* | *TF 9908 2722* |
| Syderstone | 22 | TF 8215 3262 |
| Thursford | 24 | TF 9933 3372 |
| Thursford | LH | TF 9939 3383 |
| Thursford | HGS | TF 9932 3369 |
| *Thursford* | *PB?* | *TF 9939 3370* |
| *Thursford* | *SM* | *TF 9935 3371* |
| Weasenham St Peter | HGS | TF 8559 2233 |

## Sector F

| Parish | Type | Map Ref. |
|---|---|---|
| Baconsthorpe | SM | TG 1269 3704 |
| Billingford | ATB | TG 0055 2013 |
| Booton | 22 | TG 1212 2141 |
| Cawston | SM | TG 1369 2442 |
| Corpusty | 22 | TG 1145 3016 |
| Corpusty | SM | TG 1145 3016 |
| Edgefield | SM | TG 0910 3435 |
| Gunthorpe | HGS | TG 0091 3551 |
| Heydon | HGS | TG 1124 2716 |
| *Hindolveston* | *CWM* | *TG 0400 2940* |
| *Hindolveston* | *CWM* | *TG 0359 2941* |
| Kerdiston | SM | TG 0756 2455 |
| Letheringsett | HGS | TG 0600 3875 |
| Letheringsett | SM | TG 0600 3858 |
| Letheringsett | SM | TG 0626 3871 |
| Matlaske | 22 | TG 1423 3465 |
| Matlaske | 22 | TG 1495 3477 |
| Matlaske | BHQ | TG 1450 3443 |
| *Matlaske* | *PB?* | *TG 1491 3355* |
| *Matlaske* | *PB?* | *TG 1491 3355* |
| *Matlaske* | *PB?* | *TG 1421 3464* |
| Oulton | HMG | TG 1426 2759 |
| Oulton | 27 | TG 1409 2763 |
| Reepham | 22 | TG 0682 2165 |
| Saxthorpe | 22 | TG 1146 3048 |
| *Saxthorpe* | *SM* | *TG 1135 3051* |
| *Saxthorpe* | *PB?* | *TG 1152 3040* |
| Sharrington | HGS | TG 0332 3729 |
| Sharrington | 22 | TG 0343 3648 |
| Swanton Novers | 22 | TG 0204 3260 |
| *Swanton Novers* | *PB?* | *TG 0275 3312* |
| *Swanton Novers* | *SM* | *TG 0159 2999* |
| *Thornage* | *SHB* | *TG 0586 3753* |
| West Beckham | 22 | TG 1399 3905 |
| West Beckham | 26 | TG 1395 3897 |
| West Beckham | 22 | TG 1411 3900 |
| West Beckham | 23 | TG 1423 3887 |
| West Beckham | 23 | TG 1424 3886 |
| West Beckham | SM | TG 1396 3888 |
| West Beckham | SM | TG 1401 3861 |
| Wood Dalling | 22 | TG 0890 2693 |
| Wood Norton | 22 | TG 0359 2710 |

## Sector G

| Parish | Type | Map Ref. |
|---|---|---|
| Alby with Thwaite | SM | TG 2021 3360 |
| *Aldborough* | *HGS* | *TG 1780 3432* |
| *Aldborough* | *PB?* | *TG 1795 3466* |
| Antingham | HGS | TG 2565 3209 |
| Aylsham | 22 | TG 1910 2902 |
| Aylsham | 22 | TG 1929 2867 |
| Aylsham | 24 | TG 1950 2643 |
| Aylsham | 24 | TG 1958 2643 |
| *Aylsham* | *SP* | *TG 1966 2746* |
| Aylsham | SP | TG 1979 2742 |
| Aylsham | 22 | TG 2031 2682 |
| Aylsham | LH | TG 1885 2753 |
| *Aylsham* | *PB?* | *TG 1875 2661* |
| *Aylsham* | *PB?* | *TG 1895 2705* |
| *Aylsham* | *PB?* | *TG 1926 2691* |
| *Aylsham* | *ATR* | *TG 1924 3635* |
| Bacton | W1A | TG 2994 3069 |
| Bradfield | W1A | TG 2716 3355 |
| Bradfield | W1A | TG 2715 3340 |
| Brampton | ATB | TG 2160 2537 |
| Brampton | ATB | TG 2258 2402 |
| Brampton | 22 | TG 2259 2399 |
| Buxton | ATB | TG 2370 2277 |
| Erpingham | HGS | TG 1908 3196 |
| Erpingham | SM | TG 1905 3195 |
| Felbrigg | HGS | TG 1943 3759 |
| Gimingham | 22 | TG 2950 3770 |
| Gimingham | 22 | TG 2970 3798 |
| Hanworth | W1A | TG 2130 3571 |
| Hevingham | 22 | TG 1705 2131 |
| Hevingham | 22 | TG 2173 2193 |
| Horstead | ATB | TG 2507 2163 |

| Parish | Type | Map Ref. |
|---|---|---|
| *Matlaske* | *PB?* | *TG 1524 3446* |
| North Walsham | 22 | TG 2783 3185 |
| North Walsham | 22 | TG 2715 3121 |
| *North Walsham* | *W1A* | *TG 2857 3172* |
| *North Walsham* | *W1A* | *TG 2866 3174* |
| North Walsham | HGS | TG 2945 3132 |
| North Walsham | 22 | TG 2955 3132 |
| North Walsham | W1A | TG 2968 3131 |
| North Walsham | W1A | TG 2970 3132 |
| North Walsham | ST | TG 2961 3132 |
| *North Walsham* | *SM* | *TG 2849 3155* |
| *North Walsham* | *SM* | *TG 2849 3155* |
| *North Walsham* | *PB?* | *TG 2861 3192* |
| *North Walsham* | *SM* | *TG 2861 3192* |
| North Walsham | ATR | TG 2862 3196 |
| Oulton | 27 | TG 1501 2780 |
| *Oulton* | *22* | *TG 1530 2782* |
| Scottow | 22 | TG 2650 2359 |
| Scottow | 22 | TG 2656 2195 |
| Scottow | PBX | TG 2683 2207 |
| Scottow | 25 | TG 2723 2206 |
| Scottow | 22 | TG 2750 2115 |
| Scottow | 22 | TG 2740 2116 |
| Scottow | PBX | TG 2745 2288 |
| *Thorpe Market* | *SM* | *TG 2420 3550* |
| *Thorpe Market* | *SM* | *TG 2420 3550* |
| Thorpe Market | W1A | TG 2409 3439 |
| Thorpe Market | W1A | TG 2410 3538 |
| *Trimingham* | *PB?* | *TG 2815 3864* |
| *Trimingham* | *CDL* | *TG 2835 3874* |

## Sector H

| Parish | Type | Map Ref. |
|---|---|---|
| Bacton | W1A | TG 3001 3060 |
| Bacton | 22 | TG 3295 3261 |
| Bacton | SM | TG 3387 3422 |
| Bacton | 24 | TG 3388 3418 |
| Bacton | W1A | TG 3390 3360 |
| *Bacton* | *W1A* | *TG 3397 3313* |
| Bacton | SM | TG 3408 3407 |
| Bacton | 22 | TG 3411 3408 |
| Bacton | 22 | TG 3444 3375 |
| Bacton | L | TG 3481 3355 |
| Bacton | CSP | TG 3475 3328 |
| Bacton | SM | TG 3476 3327 |
| Bacton | L | TG 3466 3324 |
| Bacton | 22 | TG 3465 3315 |
| Bacton | SM | TG 3468 3317 |
| Bacton | SM | TG 3481 3332 |
| *Bacton* | *OP* | *TG 3335 3486* |
| *Bacton* | *PB?* | *TG 3389 3447* |
| *Bacton* | *GE* | *TG 3390 3445* |
| *Bacton* | *ATB* | *TG 3398 3438* |
| *Bacton* | *PB?* | *TG 3419 3426* |
| *Bacton* | *ATB* | *TG 3420 3423* |
| *Bacton* | *PB?* | *TG 3496 3367* |
| *Catfield* | *PB?* | *TG 3980 2280* |
| Dilham | 22 | TG 3351 2654 |
| Dilham | 22 | TG 3375 2586 |
| Happisburgh | 22 | TG 3853 3062 |
| Happisburgh | 22 | TG 3881 3050 |
| Happisburgh | 22 | TG 3913 3023 |
| Happisburgh | 22 | TG 3681 3133 |
| Happisburgh | SM | TG 3680 3133 |
| Happisburgh | 27 | TG 3742 3146 |
| Happisburgh | 22 | TG 3744 3175 |
| Happisburgh | CB | TG 3750 3754 |
| *Happisburgh* | *22* | *TG 3740 3171* |
| Happisburgh | SM | TG 3749 3173 |
| Happisburgh | SM | TG 3752 3171 |
| Happisburgh | HMG | TG 3800 3127 |
| Happisburgh | 22 | TG 3826 3117 |
| *Happisburgh* | *CB* | *TG 3850 3098* |
| Happisburgh | 22 | TG 3978 2975 |
| Hempstead | 22 | TG 4042 2881 |
| Hempstead | ATB | TG 4104 2651 |
| Hickling | WM | TG 4121 2470 |
| *Hickling* | *CWM* | *TG 4141 2465* |
| *Hickling* | *PB?* | *TG 4200 2300* |
| Honing | 22 | TG 3152 2741 |
| Honing | 24 | TG 3155 2722 |
| Honing | 24 | TG 3255 2715 |
| Honing | SM | TG 3265 2713 |
| *Honing* | *PB?* | *TG 3279 2720* |
| Honing | 22 | TG 3278 2682 |
| *Horsey* | *PB?* | *TG 4643 2429* |
| *Horsey* | *PB?* | *TG 4650 2410* |
| Horsey | 24 | TG 4667 2394 |
| *Horsey* | *PB?* | *TG 4645 2428* |
| *Horsey* | *PB?* | *TG 4647 2427* |
| *Horsey* | *24* | *TG 4669 2395* |
| *Horsey* | *PB?* | *TG 4690 2370* |
| Ingham | LH | TG 3936 2610 |
| *Keswick* | *PB?* | *TG 3537 3332* |
| *Lessingham* | *PB?* | *TG 3964 3005* |
| Lessingham | 22 | TG 4030 2962 |
| Lessingham | 22 | TG 4120 2895 |
| Lessingham | 22 | TG 4129 2871 |
| Lessingham | 22 | TG 4154 2866 |
| Lessingham | HMG | TG 4171 2853 |

| Parish | Type | Map Ref. |
|---|---|---|
| Lessingham | 22 | TG 4194 2810 |
| *Lessingham* | *PB?* | *TG 3977 3000* |
| *Lessingham* | *SM* | *TG 3979 2997* |
| *Lessingham* | *PB?* | *TG 3980 2996* |
| *Lessingham* | *ATB* | *TG 3979 2994* |
| *Lessingham* | *PB?* | *TG 3989 2992* |
| *Lessingham* | *PB?* | *TG 4132 2888* |
| *Lessingham* | *PB?* | *TG 4153 2871* |
| *Lessingham* | *GE* | *TG 4181 2846* |
| *Lessingham* | *PB?* | *TG 3949 2962* |
| Mundesley | CB | TG 3080 3719 |
| Mundesley | 24 | TG 3073 3630 |
| Mundesley | SM | TG 3074 3630 |
| Mundesley | ATR | TG 3081 3710 |
| Mundesley | 24 | TG 3142 3620 |
| Mundesley | 24 | TG 3148 3650 |
| Mundesley | ATB | TG 3130 3690 |
| *Mundesley* | *PB?* | *TG 3169 3645* |
| North Walsham | HGS | TG 3000 3050 |
| North Walsham | W1A | TG 3078 2953 |
| North Walsham | W1A | TG 3083 2960 |
| North Walsham | 20 | TG 3086 2942 |
| North Walsham | 22 | TG 3099 2969 |
| North Walsham | 22 | TG 3060 2825 |
| *Paston* | *PB?* | *TG 3322 3499* |
| Sea Palling | W1A | TG 4218 2691 |
| *Sea Palling* | *22* | *TG 4300 2761* |
| *Sea Palling* | *SM* | *TG 4299 2762* |
| *Sea Palling* | *SM* | *TG 4301 2760* |
| *Sea Palling* | *PB?* | *TG 4288 2761* |
| *Sea Palling* | *PB?* | *TG 4315 2743* |
| *Sea Palling* | *PB?* | *TG 4317 2741* |
| *Sea Palling* | *PB?* | *TG 4319 2738* |
| *Sea Palling* | *PB?* | *TG 4329 2730* |
| *Sea Palling* | *PB?* | *TG 4339 2727* |
| Smallburgh | 24 | TG 3422 2470 |
| Smallburgh | 20 | TG 3470 2488 |
| Smallburgh | 22 | TG 3492 2472 |
| *Smallburgh* | *SM* | *TG 3489 2478* |
| *Smallburgh* | *SM* | *TG 3491 2478* |
| *Somerton* | *24* | *TG 4686 2017* |
| Stalham | W1A | TG 3491 2496 |
| *Stalham* | *PB?* | *TG 3480 2490* |
| *Stalham* | *W1A* | *TG 3485 2492* |
| *Stalham* | *PB?* | *TG 3675 2525* |
| *Stalham* | *PB?* | *TG 3670 2520* |
| *Stalham* | *SM* | *TG 3740 2512* |
| Stalham | SM | TG 3768 2459 |
| Trunch | W1A | TG 3029 3596 |
| Walcott | 22 | TG 3499 3228 |

| Parish | Type | Map Ref. |
|---|---|---|
| Walcott | 22 | TG 3546 3258 |
| Walcott | ATB | TG 3568 3325 |
| Walcott | 22 | TG 3607 3236 |
| Walcott | 22 | TG 3683 3169 |
| Walcott | SM | TG 3590 3291 |
| Walcott | SM | TG 3590 3291 |
| *Walcott* | *PB?* | *TG 3591 3299* |
| *Walcott* | *ATB* | *TG 3395 3396* |
| *Walcott* | *ATB* | *TG 3672 3241* |
| *Walcott* | *22* | *TG 3707 3208* |
| Waxham | 24 | TG 4414 2640 |
| Waxham | 24 | TG 4419 2639 |
| *Waxham* | *PB?* | *TG 4398 2669* |
| *Waxham* | *24* | *TG 4423 2645* |
| Winterton | ATB | TG 4849 2175 |
| *Winterton* | *PB?* | *TG 4918 2090* |
| Worstead | 22 | TG 3127 2759 |

## Sector I

| Parish | Type | Map Ref. |
|---|---|---|
| Denver | 24 | TF 5856 0093 |
| Downham West | 24 | TF 5750 0123 |
| Downham West | 24 | TF 5759 0140 |
| Downham West | 24 | TF 5932 0153 |
| Downham West | SM | TF 5996 0325 |
| Downham West | SM | TF 5968 0292 |
| Downham West | SM | TF 5954 0295 |
| Downham West | SM | TF 5987 0335 |
| Marshland St James | 22 | TF 5390 0586 |
| Nordelph | 28 | TF 5446 0097 |
| Nordelph | 24 | TF 5522 0099 |
| Nordelph | HGS | TF 5531 0082 |
| Nordelph | 28 | TF 5541 0128 |
| Nordelph | 28 | TF 5551 0098 |
| Nordelph | 24 | TF 5577 0133 |
| Nordelph | HGS | TF 5582 0097 |
| Nordelph | 24 | TF 5587 0104 |
| Nordelph | 24 | TF 5664 0104 |
| *Outwell* | *22* | *TF 5135 0365* |
| Outwell | HGS | TF 5394 0475 |
| Upwell | ATB | TF 5054 0029 |
| Upwell | SM | TF 5064 0025 |
| Upwell | 28 | TF 5064 0026 |
| *Upwell* | *PB?* | *TF 5096 0054* |
| Upwell | 24 | TF 5197 0066 |
| Upwell | 24 | TF 5278 0077 |
| Upwell | 24 | TF 5361 0088 |
| Upwell | ATR | TF 5055 0036 |
| Terrington St John | 22 | TF 5330 1569 |
| Tilney St Lawrence | 22 | TF 5656 1176 |

| Parish | Type | Map Ref. |
|---|---|---|
| Walsoken | 22 | TF 4611 1174 |
| Wiggenhall St Ger. | SM | TF 5790 1399 |
| Wiggenhall St Ger. | SM | TF 5875 1395 |

## Sector J

| Parish | Type | Map Ref. |
|---|---|---|
| Barton Bendish | HGS | TF 7086 0691 |
| *Barton Bendish* | *GP* | *TF 7113 0530* |
| Barton Bendish | 22 | TF 7190 0462 |
| Barton Bendish | 22 | TF 7240 0480 |
| Beachamwell | 22 | TF 7444 0660 |
| *Cockley Cley* | *AW* | *TF 7970 0461* |
| Cockley Cley | AW | TF 7972 0435 |
| *Cockley Cley* | *AW* | *TF 7991 0463* |
| Denver | 22 | TF 6135 0217 |
| Denver | 22 | TF 6175 0095 |
| East Walton | 22 | TF 7416 1642 |
| East Winch | 22 | TF 6986 1594 |
| Fincham | 22 | TF 6910 0610 |
| King's Lynn | ATB | TF 6264 1877 |
| King's Lynn | SM | TF 6290 1990 |
| King's Lynn | ATR | TF 6247 1972 |
| King's Lynn | SM | TF 6294 1993 |
| Marham | 22 | TF 7222 1010 |
| Marham | 22 | TF 7245 1005 |
| Marham | 22 | TF 7245 1025 |
| Marham | 22 | TF 7269 1080 |
| Narborough | SM | TF 7455 1321 |
| Narford | ATR | TF 7645 1445 |
| Pentney | SM | TF 7008 1214 |
| Pentney | 22 | TF 7478 1367 |
| Pentney | 22 | TF 7480 1380 |
| *Pentney* | *PB?* | *TF 7498 1394* |
| Stowbridge | ATB | TF 6021 0700 |
| Stradsett | 22 | TF 6635 0502 |
| Stradsett | 22 | TF 6649 0495 |
| *West Dereham* | *GP* | *TF 6720 0210* |

## Sector K

| Parish | Type | Map Ref. |
|---|---|---|
| Bradenham | HGS | TF 9300 0845 |
| *Cockley Cley* | *AW* | *TF 8035 0472* |
| *East Dereham* | *AW* | *TF 9851 1486* |
| *East Dereham* | *PB?* | *TF 9958 1352* |
| East Dereham | 22 | TF 9939 1318 |
| East Dereham | SM | TF 9991 1373 |
| *East Dereham* | *SM* | *TF 9943 1348* |
| East Dereham | 22 | TF 9882 1251 |
| East Dereham | SM | TF 9846 1351 |
| *East Dereham* | *PB?* | *TF 9845 1350* |
| *East Dereham* | *SM* | *TF 9922 1380* |
| *East Dereham* | *SM* | *TF 9923 1381* |
| *Fransham* | *PB?* | *TF 9007 1230* |
| *Griston* | *PH* | *TF 9455 0054* |
| *Griston* | *PH* | *TF 9505 0033* |
| Griston | 22 | TF 9514 0049 |
| Hilborough | 22 | TF 8170 0174 |
| Hilborough | 22 | TF 8330 0001 |
| *Hoe* | *PB?* | *TF 9852 1515* |
| Hoe | 22 | TF 9925 1765 |
| Hoe | 22 | TF 9928 1624 |
| Hoe | 22 | TF 9930 1851 |
| Hoe | 22 | TF 9945 1900 |
| Hoe | 22 | TF 9976 1939 |
| Hoe | SM | TF 9976 1940 |
| Holme Hale | 22 | TF 8896 0690 |
| Little Dunham | 22 | TF 8721 1195 |
| *North Pickenham* | *PB?* | *TF 8397 0627* |
| Scarning | 22 | TF 9659 1262 |
| Scoulton | 22 | TF 9687 0124 |
| Sporle | 22 | TF 8215 1117 |
| *Swaffham* | *PB?* | *TF 8127 0833* |
| Swaffham | 22 | TF 8162 0955 |
| *Swaffham* | *PB?* | *TF 8162 0920* |
| *Swaffham* | *PB?* | *TF 8215 0830* |
| Swaffham | 22 | TF 8324 0908 |
| Swaffham | SM | TF 8209 0836 |
| *Swaffham* | *SM* | *TF 8135 0958* |
| *Swaffham* | *PB?* | *TF 8278 0980* |
| *Swaffham* | *PB?* | *TF 8195 0956* |
| Watton | 22 | TF 9223 0100 |
| Watton | PBX | TF 9275 0069 |

## Sector L

| Parish | Type | Map Ref. |
|---|---|---|
| Barnham Broom | HGS | TG 0808 0751 |
| Bawburgh | 22 | TG 1425 0812 |
| Easthaugh | 22 | TG 0881 1723 |
| East Tuddenham | 22 | TG 0680 1185 |
| *Great Witchingham* | *CWM* | *TG 1015 1822* |
| Great Witchingham | ATB | TG 1022 1823 |
| *Hingham* | *PB?* | *TG 0140 0130* |
| North Elmham | SM | TG 0046 2019 |
| *North Elmham* | *SM* | *TG 0051 2016* |
| *North Tuddenham* | *PB?* | *TG 0180 1390* |
| Pockthorpe | ATB | TG 0719 1781 |
| Ringland | ATB | TG 1415 1366 |

| Parish | Type | Map Ref. |
|---|---|---|
| Ringland | HGS | TG 1395 1374 |
| Runhall | 22 | TG 0542 0676 |
| Swanton Morley | PH | TG 0010 1900 |
| Swanton Morley | PH | TG 0011 1850 |
| *Swanton Morley* | *PH* | *TG 0020 1820* |
| Swanton Morley | 22 | TG 0049 1940 |
| Swanton Morley | 22 | TG 0059 1792 |
| Swanton Morley | SM | TG 0205 1858 |
| Swanton Morley | SM | TG 0203 1859 |
| Weston Longville | BHQ | TG 1059 1453 |
| Wymondham | 22 | TG 0992 0116 |
| Wymondham | 22 | TG 1010 0145 |
| Wymondham | SM | TG 1057 0138 |

## Sector M

| Parish | Type | Map Ref. |
|---|---|---|
| *Brundall* | *PB?* | *TG 3295 0850* |
| Catton | 27 | TG 2251 1285 |
| *Catton* | *PB?* | *TG 2390 1175* |
| Catton | SM | TG 2331 1198 |
| Costessey | ATB | TG 1953 1032 |
| Earlham | SM | TG 1924 0823 |
| Frettenham | 22 | TG 2381 1727 |
| Hellesdon | ATB | TG 1985 1103 |
| Hellesdon | ATR | TG 1995 1115 |
| Hellesdon | 24 | TG 2005 1117 |
| Hellington | 22 | TG 3194 0224 |
| *Horsham St Faith* | *27* | *TG 2130 1292* |
| Horsham St Faith | PH | TG 2141 1356 |
| Horsham St Faith | PH | TG 2204 1340 |
| Horsham St Faith | PH | TG 2244 1369 |
| Horstead | 24 | TG 2646 1990 |
| *Horstead* | *24* | *TG 2644 1958* |
| Keswick | HGS | TG 2124 0509 |
| *Lakenham* | *PB?* | *TG 2420 0715* |
| Norwich | HGS | TG 2401 0832 |
| Norwich | HGS | TG 2401 0832 |
| Poringland | 22 | TG 2610 0254 |
| Poringland | HGS | TG 2732 0155 |
| Postwick | 22 | TG 2879 0689 |
| *Sprowston* | *22* | *TG 2631 1199* |
| *Stoke Holy Cross* | *22* | *TG 2480 0230* |
| *Thorpe St Andrew* | *22* | *TG 2619 1005* |
| *Thorpe St Andrew* | *22* | *TG 2686 0790* |
| Thorpe St Andrew | ATB | TG 2737 0956 |
| Thorpe St Andrew | ATB | TG 2774 0890 |
| Thorpe St Andrew | ATB | TG 2730 0855 |
| Thorpe St Andrew | ATB | TG 2750 0866 |
| Thorpe St Andrew | ATD | TG 2756 0841 |
| Thorpe St Andrew | ATB | TG 2756 0847 |
| Thorpe St Andrew | ATB | TG 2786 0840 |
| *Thorpe St Andrew* | *PB?* | *TG 2742 0875* |
| Thurton | SM | TG 3350 0045 |
| Upper Stoke | PBX | TG 2515 0263 |
| Upper Stoke | LAA | TG 2515 0263 |
| *Upper Stoke* | *PBX* | *TG 2525 0275* |
| Upper Stoke | PBX | TG 2526 0254 |
| *Upper Stoke* | *PBX* | *TG 2534 0270* |
| Upper Stoke | 22 | TG 2528 0321 |
| *Upper Stoke* | *22* | *TG 2480 0230* |
| Wroxham | 22 | TG 2965 1689 |
| *Wroxham* | *PB?* | *TG 3015 1805* |

## Sector N

| Parish | Type | Map Ref. |
|---|---|---|
| Acle | CSP | TG 4021 1063 |
| Acle | LH | TG 4021 1050 |
| *Acle* | *22* | *TG 4070 1083* |
| Acle | 22 | TG 4066 1062 |
| *Acle* | *22* | *TG 4111 1071* |
| Acle | SM | TG 4130 1166 |
| Acle | SM | TG 4148 1163 |
| Acle | SM | TG 4147 1154 |
| *Acle* | *SM* | *TG 4131 1162* |
| Acle | 22 | TG 4114 0996 |
| Beighton | 22 | TG 3940 0715 |
| Belton | ATB | TG 4975 0082 |
| *Bradwell* | *ATB* | *TG 5099 0510* |
| *Bradwell* | *PB?* | *TG 5117 0429* |
| Buckenham | HGS | TG 3523 9590 |
| *Burgh Castle* | *W1A* | *TG 4830 0630* |
| *Caister-on-Sea* | *SM* | *TG 5227 1360* |
| *Caister-on-Sea* | *22* | *TG 5227 1359* |
| *Caister-on-Sea* | *ATB* | *TG 5230 1320* |
| Caister-on-Sea | 24 | TG 5193 1272 |
| Caister-on-Sea | 24 | TG 5176 1268 |
| *Caister-on-Sea* | *PB?* | *TG 5150 1240* |
| Caister-on-Sea | 20 | TG 5259 2441 |
| *Caister-on-Sea* | *PB?* | *TG 5267 1227* |
| *Caister-on-Sea* | *PB?* | *TG 5268 1225* |
| *Caister-on-Sea* | *PB?* | *TG 5292 1166* |
| *Caister-on-Sea* | *PB?* | *TG 5295 1139* |
| *Caister-on-Sea* | *PB?* | *TG 5302 1108* |
| *Caister-on-Sea* | *PB?* | *TG 5303 1105* |
| *Caister-on-Sea* | *PB?* | *TG 5314 1062* |
| *Caister-on-Sea* | *PB?* | *TG 5314 1060* |
| *Caister-on-Sea* | *SM* | *TG 5311 1050* |
| Caister-on-Sea | 22 | TG 5241 1059 |
| *Caister-on-Sea* | *SM* | *TG 5306 1101* |
| Fleggburgh | HGS | TG 4520 1391 |

| Parish | Type | Map Ref. |
|---|---|---|
| *Great Yarmouth* | *22* | *TG 5307 1001* |
| *Great Yarmouth* | *CDL* | *TG 5320 1010* |
| *Great Yarmouth* | *W1A* | *TG 4909 0742* |
| Great Yarmouth | W1B | TG 5053 0889 |
| Great Yarmouth | W1B | TG 5049 0921 |
| Great Yarmouth | 24 | TG 5155 0683 |
| *Great Yarmouth* | *PB?* | *TG 5165 0817* |
| *Great Yarmouth* | *PB?* | *TG 5190 0640* |
| *Great Yarmouth* | *PB?* | *TG 5190 0805* |
| *Great Yarmouth* | *22* | *TG 5201 0542* |
| *Great Yarmouth* | *22* | *TG 5203 0522* |
| *Great Yarmouth* | *PB?* | *TG 5220 0215* |
| *Great Yarmouth* | *PB?* | *TG 5210 0590* |
| *Great Yarmouth* | *PB?* | *TG 5212 0639* |
| *Great Yarmouth* | *PB?* | *TG 5220 0325* |
| *Great Yarmouth* | *PB?* | *TG 5220 0617* |
| Great Yarmouth | 24 | TG 5138 0731 |
| *Great Yarmouth* | *PB?* | *TG 5241 0587* |
| *Great Yarmouth* | *PB?* | *TG 5240 0610* |
| *Great Yarmouth* | *SM* | *TG 5278 0180* |
| *Great Yarmouth* | *SM* | *TG 5280 0198* |
| *Great Yarmouth* | *PB?* | *TG 5285 0321* |
| *Great Yarmouth* | *SM* | *TG 5290 0320* |
| *Great Yarmouth* | *PB?* | *TG 5294 0320* |
| *Great Yarmouth* | *GE* | *TG 5300 0341* |
| *Great Yarmouth* | *SM* | *TG 5306 0197* |
| *Great Yarmouth* | *HAA* | *TG 5310 0125* |
| *Great Yarmouth* | *CB* | *TG 5312 0205* |
| *Great Yarmouth* | *SM* | *TG 5314 0168* |
| *Great Yarmouth* | *CDL* | *TG 5316 0222* |
| *Great Yarmouth* | *28* | *TG 5295 0343* |
| *Great Yarmouth* | *CDL* | *TG 5320 0162* |
| *Great Yarmouth* | *PB?* | *TG 5320 0360* |
| *Great Yarmouth* | *PB?* | *TG 5321 0303* |
| *Great Yarmouth* | *22* | *TG 5317 0155* |
| *Great Yarmouth* | *CB* | *TG 5338 0055* |
| *Great Yarmouth* | *CB* | *TG 5341 0366* |
| *Great Yarmouth* | *CDL* | *TG 5341 0366* |
| *Great Yarmouth* | *PB?* | *TG 5294 0327* |
| *Great Yarmouth* | *PB?* | *TG 5308 0238* |
| Great Yarmouth | 24 | TG 5108 0683 |
| Great Yarmouth | 24 | TG 5123 0673 |
| Great Yarmouth | 24 | TG 5131 0665 |
| Great Yarmouth | 24 | TG 5140 0682 |
| Great Yarmouth | 24 | TG 5181 0674 |
| Great Yarmouth | 24 | TG 5185 0662 |
| Great Yarmouth | 24 | TG 5208 0632 |
| *Great Yarmouth* | *CDL* | *TG 5338 0388* |
| *Great Yarmouth* | *CDL* | *TG 5338 0390* |
| *Great Yarmouth* | *CB* | *TG 5338 0395* |
| *Great Yarmouth* | *PB?* | *TG 5320 0495* |
| *Great Yarmouth* | *PB?* | *TG 5320 0525* |
| *Great Yarmouth* | *PB?* | *TG 5306 0580* |
| *Great Yarmouth* | *PB?* | *TG 5316 0513* |
| *Great Yarmouth* | *PB?* | *TG 5320 0518* |
| *Great Yarmouth* | *PB?* | *TG 5320 0523* |
| *Great Yarmouth* | *PB?* | *TG 5315 0622* |
| *Great Yarmouth* | *GE* | *TG 5317 0642* |
| *Great Yarmouth* | *PB?* | *TG 5320 0660* |
| *Great Yarmouth* | *SM* | *TG 5332 0750* |
| *Great Yarmouth* | *PB?* | *TG 5325 0672* |
| *Great Yarmouth* | *CDL* | *TG 5335 0672* |
| *Great Yarmouth* | *PB?* | *TG 5316 0678* |
| *Great Yarmouth* | *SM* | *TG 5316 0683* |
| *Great Yarmouth* | *PB?* | *TG 5316 0688* |
| *Great Yarmouth* | *PB?* | *TG 5316 0710* |
| *Great Yarmouth* | *PB?* | *TG 5316 0720* |
| *Great Yarmouth* | *SM* | *TG 5316 0735* |
| *Great Yarmouth* | *PB?* | *TG 5220 0750* |
| *Great Yarmouth* | *PB?* | *TG 5218 0752* |
| *Great Yarmouth* | *SM* | *TG 5320 0680* |
| *Great Yarmouth* | *PB?* | *TG 5314 0720* |
| *Great Yarmouth* | *SM* | *TG 5320 0750* |
| *Great Yarmouth* | *PB?* | *TG 5312 0922* |
| *Great Yarmouth* | *PB?* | *TG 5315 0776* |
| *Great Yarmouth* | *PB?* | *TG 5327 0770* |
| *Great Yarmouth* | *PB?* | *TG 5327 0776* |
| *Great Yarmouth* | *PB?* | *TG 5321 0776* |
| *Great Yarmouth* | *GE* | *TG 5321 0784* |
| *Great Yarmouth* | *PB?* | *TG 5315 0789* |
| *Great Yarmouth* | *PB?* | *TG 5321 0815* |
| *Great Yarmouth* | *SM* | *TG 5321 0840* |
| *Great Yarmouth* | *CDL* | *TG 5322 0851* |
| *Great Yarmouth* | *SM* | *TG 5321 0857* |
| *Great Yarmouth* | *SM* | *TG 5315 0862* |
| *Great Yarmouth* | *PB?* | *TG 5322 0863* |
| *Great Yarmouth* | *PB?* | *TG 5315 0879* |
| *Great Yarmouth* | *PB?* | *TG 5312 0922* |
| *Great Yarmouth* | *PB?* | *TG 5319 0922* |
| *Great Yarmouth* | *PB?* | *TG 5312 0935* |
| *Great Yarmouth* | *PB?* | *TG 5312 0949* |
| *Great Yarmouth* | *PB?* | *TG 5313 0969* |
| *Great Yarmouth* | *CDL* | *TG 5322 0970* |
| *Great Yarmouth* | *CB* | *TG 5313 0990* |
| Great Yarmouth | 22 | TG 5194 0790 |
| *Great Yarmouth* | *DP* | *TG 5289 0629* |
| *Great Yarmouth* | *DP* | *TG 5277 0630* |
| Halvergate | CSP | TG 4180 0730 |
| Halvergate | HGS | TG 4260 0696 |
| Halvergate | 22 | TG 4269 0696 |

| Parish | Type | Map Ref. |
|---|---|---|
| Halvergate | CSP | TG 4419 0899 |
| Hemsby | 22 | TG 5096 1767 |
| Hemsby | 24 | TG 4993 1781 |
| Hemsby | SM | TG 5068 1744 |
| Hemsby | 2/20 | TG 5069 1733 |
| Hemsby | ATB | TG 5066 1725 |
| Hemsby | 24 | TG 5020 1756 |
| Hemsby | 24 | TG 4970 1704 |
| *Hemsby* | *22* | *TG 5094 1692* |
| Hemsby | GP | TG 4990 1690 |
| *Hemsby* | *24* | *TG 5040 1690* |
| Hemsby | 22 | TG 5108 1646 |
| Hemsby | ATB | TG 5107 1647 |
| Hopton-on-Sea | ATB | TG 5042 0051 |
| Hopton-on-Sea | ATB | TG 5096 0055 |
| Hopton-on-Sea | ATB | TG 5147 0068 |
| Hopton-on-Sea | 22 | TG 5179 0094 |
| Hopton-on-Sea | 22 | TG 5252 0156 |
| Hopton-on-Sea | 22 | TG 5255 0119 |
| *Hopton-on-Sea* | *22* | *TG 5347 0024* |
| Hopton-on-Sea | SM | TG 5148 0082 |
| Hopton-on-Sea | SM | TG 5175 0095 |
| Hopton-on-Sea | SM | TG 5180 0100 |
| Hopton-on-Sea | SM | TG 5228 0111 |
| Hopton-on-Sea | SM | TG 5237 0112 |
| Hopton-on-Sea | SM | TG 5255 0118 |
| *Hopton-on-Sea* | *PB?* | *TG 5350 9965* |
| Ludham | SM | TG 3718 1710 |
| Ludham | CSP | TG 3718 1721 |
| Ludham | SM | TG 3715 1715 |
| Ludham | HGS | TG 3875 1825 |
| Ludham | 22 | TG 3894 1745 |
| Ludham | PBX | TG 3885 1943 |
| Ludham | SP | TG 3989 1987 |
| Ludham | PBX | TG 4020 1893 |
| Mautby | 22 | TG 4605 1212 |
| Mautby | HAA | TG 4870 1095 |
| *Ormesby St Marg.* | *SM* | *TG 5214 1412* |
| *Ormesby St Marg.* | *22* | *TG 5214 1411* |
| *Ormesby St Marg.* | *PB?* | *TG 5089 1591* |
| *Ormesby St Marg.* | *WM* | *TG 5115 1621* |
| *Ormesby St Marg.* | *PB?* | *TG 5150 1550* |
| Ormesby St Marg. | SM | TG 5151 1549 |
| Ormesby St Marg. | 24 | TG 5153 1475 |
| Ormesby St Marg. | SM | TG 5152 1463 |
| Ormesby St Marg. | 22 | TG 5192 1468 |
| Potter Heigham | SM | TG 4201 1835 |
| Potter Heigham | SM | TG 4210 1845 |
| Potter Heigham | SM | TG 4182 1849 |
| *Potter Heigham* | *SM* | *TG 4185 1845* |

| Parish | Type | Map Ref. |
|---|---|---|
| Reedham | HGS | TG 4220 0176 |
| Rollesby | 22 | TG 4435 1595 |
| *Scratby* | *22* | *TG 5130 1586* |
| Upton & Fishley | 22 | TG 3957 1156 |
| Upton & Fishley | 22 | TG 3986 1114 |
| West Caister | HAA | TG 5035 1136 |
| *West Caister* | *WM* | *TG 5120 1176* |
| West Caister | 22 | TG 5172 1025 |
| West Caister | 22 | TG 5211 1054 |
| *West Caister* | *PB?* | *TG 5235 1060* |
| Winterton | SM | TG 4971 1970 |
| *Winterton* | *EH* | *TG 4977 1966* |
| Winterton | ATB | TG 4991 1972 |
| *Winterton* | *PB?* | *TG 4992 1987* |
| *Winterton* | *CDL* | *TG 4999 1949* |
| *Winterton* | *SM* | *TG 4970 1940* |
| *Winterton* | *PB?* | *TG 4971 1939* |
| Winterton | EH | TG 4994 1329 |
| Winterton | CB | TG 4979 1921 |
| *Winterton* | *SM* | *TG 4965 1918* |
| *Winterton* | *SM* | *TG 4969 1907* |
| *Winterton* | *PB?* | *TG 4972 1907* |
| *Winterton* | *PB?* | *TG 5005 1921* |
| *Winterton* | *CDL* | *TG 5008 1919* |
| *Winterton* | *PB?* | *TG 5005 1913* |
| *Winterton* | *PB?* | *TG 5009 1916* |
| Winterton | 22 | TG 5030 1915 |
| Winterton | 22 | TG 5035 1850 |
| Winterton | SM | TG 4975 1973 |
| Winterton | SM | TG 5030 1925 |
| Winterton | SM | TG 5030 1905 |

## Sector O - Nil

## Sector P

| Parish | Type | Map Ref. |
|---|---|---|
| Cranwich | 22 | TL 7690 9228 |
| *Denver* | *PB?* | *TL 5907 9865* |
| Didlington | 22 | TL 7935 9698 |
| Feltwell | 26 | TL 7017 9045 |
| Feltwell | 26 | TL 7054 8954 |
| Fordham | HGS | TL 6195 9866 |
| *Fordham* | *PB?* | *TL 6220 9875* |
| Fordham | SM | TL 6210 9880 |
| Fordham | 22 | TL 6309 9818 |
| Hilgay | SM | TL 6045 9698 |
| Hilgay | 24 | TL 6047 9700 |
| Hilgay | 28 | TL 6038 9717 |
| Hilgay | 24 | TL 6016 9768 |

| Parish | Type | Map Ref. |
|---|---|---|
| Hockwold | 26 | TL 7009 8833 |
| Hockwold | 26 | TL 7009 8881 |
| Hockwold | BHQ | TL 7015 8882 |
| Hockwold | 22 | TL 7031 8802 |
| Methwold | 22 | TL 6650 9237 |
| Methwold | 26 | TL 7367 9480 |
| Methwold | 26 | TL 7369 9481 |
| Methwold | LAA | TL 7396 9302 |
| Northwold | SM | TL 7700 9647 |
| Southery | 28 | TL 6089 9186 |
| Southery | 22 | TL 6143 9129 |
| Southery | 24 | TL 6136 9349 |
| Southery | 24 | TL 6035 9623 |
| *Stoke Ferry* | *SM* | *TL 7079 9951* |
| Weeting | 22 | TL 7822 8705 |

## Sector Q

| Parish | Type | Map Ref. |
|---|---|---|
| Bridgham | 22 | TL 9480 8650 |
| *Caston* | *PB?* | *TL 9777 9659* |
| *Croxton* | *PB?* | *TL 8571 8670* |
| Croxton | 22 | TL 8730 8508 |
| Croxton | 22 | TL 8750 8508 |
| East Harling | SP | TL 9895 8665 |
| Hilborough | 22 | TL 8331 9996 |
| Hilborough | 22 | TL 8424 9751 |
| Hilborough | 22 | TL 8401 9988 |
| Hilborough | LAA | TL 8444 9918 |
| Hilborough | 22 | TL 8447 9913 |
| Hilborough | BHQ | TL 8447 9915 |
| Hilborough | 22 | TL 8474 9957 |
| Hilborough | PB? | TL 8515 9813 |
| Kilverstone | 22 | TL 9023 8672 |
| Langford | 22 | TL 8390 9625 |
| Merton | PB? | TL 8840 9760 |
| Merton | HGS | TL 9235 9887 |
| *Shropham* | *SL* | *TL 9725 9190* |
| Thetford | SM | TL 8650 8331 |
| Thetford | 22 | TL 8678 8307 |
| Thetford | 22 | TL 8691 8374 |
| Thetford | 22 | TL 8707 8253 |
| *Thetford* | *SM* | *TL 8730 8400* |
| *Thetford* | *PB?* | *TL 8745 8115* |
| *Thetford* | *SM* | *TL 8750 8240* |
| Thetford | 28 | TL 8763 8346 |
| *Thetford* | *SM* | *TL 8800 8295* |
| *Thetford* | *PB?* | *TL 8859 8142* |
| Thetford | SM | TL 8664 8288 |
| Wretham | 22 | TL 8986 8974 |
| Wretham | 2/20 | TL 8996 8974 |
| Wretham | 2/20 | TL 9111 8940 |
| Wretham | 2/20 | TL 9111 8932 |
| Wretham | 22 | TL 9117 8941 |
| Wretham | 22 | TL 9114 8928 |
| Wretham | 22 | TL 9156 9105 |

## Sector R

| Parish | Type | Map Ref. |
|---|---|---|
| *Attleborough* | *22* | *TM 0495 9525* |
| Banham | 22 | TM 0510 8710 |
| Besthorpe | PBX | TM 0630 9545 |
| *Besthorpe* | *PB?* | *TM 0440 9588* |
| Bressingham | 22 | TM 0686 8165 |
| Dickleburgh | 22 | TM 1737 8208 |
| *Diss* | *PB?* | *TM 1000 8050* |
| Diss | 22 | TM 1273 7962 |
| Diss | 22 | TM 1219 8240 |
| East Harling | 22 | TM 0082 8638 |
| Gissing | 22 | TM 1419 8746 |
| Hapton | 22 | TM 1876 9675 |
| Hargham | 22 | TM 0175 9120 |
| North Lopham | 22 | TM 0264 821 |
| Pulham Market | LH | TM 1969 8607 |
| *Pulham Market* | *PB?* | *TM 1890 8755* |
| Quidenham | LAA | TM 0089 9132 |
| Thorpe Abbotts | BHQ | TM 1904 8131 |
| Winfarthing | 22 | TM 0919 8667 |
| Wymondham | 22 | TM 0932 9677 |

## Sector S

| Parish | Type | Map Ref. |
|---|---|---|
| Alburgh | 22 | TM 2491 8727 |
| *Chedgrave* | *SM* | *TM 3539 9938* |
| Ellingham | 22 | TM 3660 9200 |
| Harleston | 22 | TM 2445 8325 |
| Harleston | SM | TM 2421 8332 |
| *Harleston* | *SM* | *TM 2465 8320* |
| *Harleston* | *BB* | *TM 2470 8390* |
| *Harleston* | *PB?* | *TM 2471 8389* |
| *Harleston* | *BB* | *TM 2485 8382* |
| Harleston | GE | TM 2492 8312 |
| *Loddon* | *22* | *TM 3649 9833* |
| Loddon | 22 | TM 3638 9779 |
| Loddon | 22 | TM 3608 9902 |
| Raveningham | 22 | TM 3945 9675 |
| Raveningham | SM | TM 3941 9672 |
| Raveningham | SM | TM 3920 9697 |
| Raveningham | SM | TM 3962 9720 |
| Shelton | 22 | TM 2235 9179 |
| Topcroft | 22 | TM 2600 9270 |

| **Parish** | **Type** | **Map Ref.** |
|---|---|---|
| **Sector T** | | |
| *Aldeby* | *22* | *TM 4251 9301* |
| Haddiscoe | 22 | TM 4525 9917 |
| Haddiscoe | W1B | TM 4559 9932 |
| Haddiscoe | 22 | TM 4599 9850 |
| Haddiscoe | 22 | TM 4601 9835 |
| Haddiscoe | SM | TM 4448 9687 |
| St Olaves | SM | TM 4607 9867 |
| Wheatacre | 22 | TM 4741 9678 |

---

## *BIBLIOGRAPHY*

---

**Titles in bold are recommended for further reading.**


Armstrong, M.J., *History and Antiquities of the County of Norfolk.* Norwich, 1781.

Baldwin, J., and Tickle, A., *Memories of Fakenham Lancaster.* Jim Baldwin Publishing, 1991.

Banse, Ewald, *Germany, Prepare for War!* Lovat Dickson, 1934.

Brooks, Peter, *Coastal Towns at War.* Poppyland Publishing, 1988.

**Brown, Ian, and others, *20th Century Defences in Britain; an introductory guide.* Council for British Archaeology, 1995.**

Cozens-Hardy, Basil, 'Norfolk Coastal Defences in 1588.' *Norfolk Archaeology,* vol 26, 1938.

Davis, Brian L., *The British Army in WW II.* Lionel Leventhall Ltd., 1990.

Dorman, Jeff, 'Norfolk and Suffolk Coast Defence Study.' *Ravelin,* no. 19, October 1989.

Fairhead, Huby, *Decoy Sites: Wartime Deception in Norfolk and Suffolk.* Huby Fairhead, 1996.

Frayn Turner, John, *Highly Explosive.* White Lion, 1974.

Gee, P.W., *A History of the Essex Yeomanry 1919-1949.* Benham and Co. Limited, 1950.

Hoare, Adrian, *Standing up to Hitler: The story of Norfolk's Home Guard and 'Secret Army' 1940-44.* Geo. R. Reeve Limited, 1997.

Innes, Graham Buchan, *British Airfield Buildings of the Second World War.* Midland Publishing Limited, 1995.

Johnson, Derek E., *East Anglia at War.* Jarrold Publishing, 1992.

Jones, R.V., *Reflections on Intelligence.* William Heinemann Limited, 1989.

**Kent, Peter, *Fortifications of East Anglia.* Terence Dalton, 1988.**

Kent, Peter, 'The Fixed Defences.' *Norfolk and Suffolk in the Great War,* ed. Gerald Gliddon, Gliddon Books, 1988.

Macrae, R.S., *Winston Churchill's Toyshop.* Kineton, 1971.

Osborne, Mike, 'Pillbox Typology.' *Loopholes: the Journal of the Pillbox Study Group,* ed. David Burridge, nos. 3-6, 8, 1993-4.

**Saunders, Andrew, *Fortress Britain: artillery fortifications in the British Isles and Ireland.* Beaufort Publishing, 1989.**

**Wills, Henry, *Pillboxes: a Study of U.K. Defences 1940.* Leo Cooper/Secker and Warburg, 1985.**